⑨ BLAZERS™ Profiles™

Written
by Kerry Eggers
Photos from
the 1990-91 Season
by Brian Drake

MW00813217

✕ GRAPHIC ARTS CENTER PUBLISHING COMPANY

To my father, John, whose spirit
will stay with me forever;
to my mother, Jean, who continues to be
a bright sparkle in my life;
to my wife, Julia, whose inspiration, love and support
have helped keep me ticking.

KERRY EGGERS

International Standard Book Number 1-55868-078-0
Library of Congress Number 91-76344
Photographs ©MCMXCI by Portland Trail Blazers
Text ©MCMXCI by Kerry Eggers
Published by Graphic Arts Center Publishing Company
P.O. Box 10306 • Portland, OR 97210 • 503/226-2402
All rights reserved. No part of this book
can be reproduced by any means
without written permission of the publisher.
President • Charles M. Hopkins
Editor-in-Chief • Douglas A. Pfeiffer
Managing Editor • Jean Andrews
Designer • Robert Reynolds
Typographer • Harrison Typesetting, Inc.
Color Separations • Wy'east Color, Inc.
Printer • Rono Graphic Communications Co.
Bindery • Lincoln & Allen
Printed and bound in the United States of America

The cover photo, taken during the 1991 Western Conference Finals with the Los Angeles Lakers, shows Portland's Clyde Drexler driving for a basket over James Worthy. ◄ ◄ The title page photo depicts Drexler taking the ball to the hoop against a player of some renown, Chicago's Michael Jordan. ◄ Coach Rick Adelman, left, consults with assistants John Wetzel, center, and Jack Schalow. ▲ As he goes up for a shot, San Antonio's Terry Cummings meets resistance in Portland's Buck Williams, Jerome Kersey, and Cliff Robinson. ►

Contents

Foreword

by Hank Hersch
Staff Writer for Sports Illustrated

Memorial Coliseum's score-board salutes the Portland Trail Blazers as the 1990-91 Pacific Division champions. Portland finished the regular season with an NBA-best record of 63-19, beginning the year with 19-1 and finishing it with a 15-1 winning streak. ▲

Getting an assignment from *Sports Illustrated* inevitably inspires a mixture of feelings—excitement and anxiety to name at least two—depending on the variables of the story I'm to cover: the quality of the city, the caliber of the event, and the cooperativeness of athletes and coaches. During the past two springs, the magazine has sent me some three thousand miles from my home in New York. I have been sent to ride the tidal wave called Blazermania, to cover Portland during the NBA Play-offs.

Let's examine the variables of that task. First, I am going to a city of lush green and (aside from Memorial Coliseum) soothing sanity, both of which are a welcome departure from downtown Manhattan. Then there is the sheer pleasure of watching basketball played for its greatest stakes before its most supportive crowd by its most explosive team. No starting five in the league can attack an opponent with as much ferocity in as many different ways. When the Trail Blazers are stealing, wheeling, and dealing, they are a beauty to behold.

The images are many: Clyde Drexler floating toward the hoop with effortless elegance, then dunking with menacing gusto; Terry Porter studying his options at the top of the key at a pace all his own, waiting to nail a three; Jerome Kersey out on the break, pursuing the play with no regard for life or limb, his or anyone else's; Kevin Duckworth pounding a dribble and shedding bodies before he drops a left-hand hook; Buck Williams going up once, twice, three times for a rebound, then heading off to the foul line for a three-point play. Individual skill is what makes the NBA so intriguing; everyone from the 12th man on up has a style all his own. Few teams blend their talents as gracefully as the Blazers.

But what makes the trip to Portland at once easy and exhilarating is the unfailing professionalism of the Blazers themselves. Each member of the organization has been direct and willing to answer tough questions after tough losses. As a rule, the NBA is not a league littered with prima donnas. But the Portland locker room has an air of levelheadedness and geniality that is rare. Not only do I sense that the players are good people by nature, but also that they are unusually committed—to each other, to winning a title, to the community. Blazermania hasn't spoiled them; instead, it has inspired them.

These are my impressions. A few pressure-filled weeks in Portland hardly qualify me as an expert; I only see a few scenes from a drama that plays for eight months every year. I don't really get a chance to know the players, especially when I am one among dozens of notebook-toting members of the media. BLAZERS PROFILES has helped bridge that gap and brought me closer to what makes the team tick. Kerry Eggers, one of the more respected writers on the NBA beat, and photographer Brian Drake have presented a group portrait of twelve driven individuals, shedding light on where they are from, what they want, and how they live.

I assure you that the next time I get sent to Portland, this book will be one of the first things I pack.

Darn Straight Herb, who has my ear when he talks (and he can talk), is a lot like any fan of the Portland Trail Blazers. He is enthralled with the way the Blazers have played over the past two seasons, when they amassed 122 regular-season victories and made back-to-back appearances in the NBA's Western Conference Finals. He appreciates Coach Rick Adelman, who has provided his players with direction without taking away the spontaneity of one of the most athletic teams. Herb's life was momentarily shattered when the Blazers' bid for a world championship fell short both years. His spirit was resilient. "The guys are still young," he said, sipping a diet soda as he lunched on chicken salad before the 1991-92 season. "They're going to hang a championship banner in Memorial Coliseum sometime soon. Darn straight."

Herb believes a team is the sum total of its parts. Over the past two seasons, he has taken care to scrutinize the Blazer players as people. He gathers information about them like a squirrel collecting acorns, gleaning tidbits about their personalities, their backgrounds, their family life, their interests. He says he could root for the Blazers even if they were losers.

He thinks Clyde Drexler has matured and grown as a person since his early years as a Blazer. He likes Terry Porter's commitment to civic and charitable causes, Buck Williams' integrity, Kevin Duckworth's candid demeanor, Danny Ainge's wit and humor, Wayne Cooper's empathy, Alaa Abdelnaby's charm and intellect.

There are a lot of similarities among the Blazer players. Most are black, many come from low-income, single-parent homes and remain close to their mothers, and several are deeply religious. Herb respects them for their differences as well. Some are outspoken and revel in the limelight, others shun it. Some have outstanding natural athletic abilities, others have made it as blue-collar types who fit into a team structure.

On the court, Herb enjoys Drexler's athleticism and grace, Jerome Kersey's hustle, Williams' toughness, Cliff Robinson's range and versatility, Porter's floor leadership and clutch play. He appreciates a team that runs on offense, prides itself on its defense, and ranks as one of the best in the NBA in rebounding and three-point shooting. "It's almost like a college team," Herb says, "in the effort they put in, and the way they give credit to one another. Darn straight."

The style of basketball the Blazers play—and the frequency of their victories—has unified the city, the state, and the region, Herb says. The Blazers have put Portland on the map. "My two cousins in New York City used to ask me how it felt to live in lumberjack land," Herb chuckles. "Now they want to come out for a visit, if I can get them tickets to a Blazer game."

Let's take an inside look at the Blazer players Herb so admires. Let's listen as they talk about their childhoods, their families, their dreams. Let's see what makes them men and what those men have done to help make the Trail Blazers a great team. Darn straight.

Introduction

The Blazers enjoy clowning *around before the shooting of their 1990-91 squad photograph. The Portland Trail Blazer players share a genuine* esprit de corps *rare on teams in professional sports.* ▲

Terry Porter stands over his 18-foot birdie putt on the ninth green at Portland's Columbia-Edgewater Country Club. Nattily attired in designer golf gear, a derby cap covering his shaved pate, Porter is a member of the Tualatin Country Club, but today he is a guest of his friend, Ron Sloy, in a stag calcutta and scramble.

With the NBA season not yet a week over, Porter, the star point guard of the Portland Trail Blazers, is only too happy to participate.

Porter sizes the putt, steps up, and drills the ball toward the hole. The ball hits the back of the cup, pops up, and plops down.

"Baby!" yells Sloy, who exchanges high-fives with his partner. "I told him not to leave that mother short."

Porter smiles. "If that'd been against the Lakers . . ." he begins, then cuts himself short.

Five days earlier, Porter's last-second, 18-foot jump shot had been just a trifle short, bouncing off the front rim and allowing the Los Angeles Lakers to escape with a 91-90 victory over the Trail Blazers in Game 6 of their best-of-seven Western Conference finals.

For the Blazers, it ended their championship dreams. For Porter, who has earned a reputation for being a player the Blazers could count on to make big plays in tough games, it was an unfitting finale to a wondrous season.

The young man—who received no college scholarship offers as a 6-1 forward out of high school, then paid his way to play for NAIA Wisconsin-Stevens Point—had arrived. Porter finally received equal billing with NBA point-guard laureates Stockton, Johnson, Thomas, and Price. In 1991, he made the NBA All-Star Game for the first time. He directed the Blazers to the league's best regular-season record, and he led them to the Western Conference finals for the second successive season.

Now, as Porter relaxed following his team's elimination, he sought perspective on both past and future.

On the past: "We fell short of winning a world championship. Had we won Game 6, I think we'd have beaten the Lakers in Game 7 and gone on to beat Chicago for the title. It's kind of frustrating when you're a shot or a couple of plays away from having a great opportunity to win it, but I think as time goes on we'll realize the kind of year we actually had. We had the best record in the league, we won the Pacific Division, we earned a lot of respect. For the second year in a row, we played into June."

On the future: "It's going to definitely make us hungrier next season. We have a great opportunity again. The nucleus of talent is really good; the young guys are coming along. With the character of this ball club, we're going to be back. I think we have six more good years left with the talent we have."

At 28, six years is probably about what the 6-3 Porter has left to play. That would mean a dozen NBA seasons, a ton of points and assists, and a special kind of appreciation for what it takes to come up through the ranks to make it to the top.

Terry Porter

Terry Porter has come a long way since his days as an unknown in college at Wisconsin-Stevens Point. He is now an All-Star and a crowd favorite in Portland. Porter waves a towel in response to an ovation given him by fans in the Coliseum, who listen to his comments as a post-game radio guest. ◄ The NBA is a rugged game. Porter uses an ice bag to relieve aches and pains. ▲

Porter brings the ball up-court against the Miami Heat. The 6-3 point guard is a savvy player who has gradually earned acclaim as one of the best at his position. He's not often called upon for rebounding duties, but Terry has a good nose for the basketball. ▲
Porter and Kevin Duckworth box out their Laker foes. ▶

It has not been an easy climb. Terry was born in Milwaukee, Wisconsin, the last of Herman and Louise Porter's six children, nine years younger than the next-youngest sibling. His father was foreman at an automobile products plant. "He's always been a blue-collar type of guy," Terry says now. Terry describes him as "easygoing, but kind of strict with us kids. We're pretty close, even though it wasn't always that way."

Terry was closer to his mother than his father. He thinks he has a lot of his mother in him and describes her as "really quiet, easy to get along with." When she died of lung and kidney failure during the 1989-90 season, Terry dedicated the season to her, writing her initials "LP" on the back of his sneakers. His only regret when the Blazers reached the NBA Finals was that she didn't live to enjoy the finals with him.

The Porters were not destitute, but money was not plentiful, not with eight mouths to feed. "If there's something between poor and middle class, that's where we were at. We always got Christmas presents. We always got by."

As he grew up, sports were a constant, and Terry played football, basketball, or baseball in the streets or at nearby Atkinson Park. He was a good kid, and having sports helped. "I really didn't get into much trouble," he recalls. "I got into playing ball."

He was a decent athlete, but not an immediate sensation. "You wouldn't have looked at me as a youngster," he says, "and thought I had stardom written all over me." It took Porter a while to find his niche in sports at South Division High. He did not go out for basketball until he was a junior, and while he made the varsity as a rugged 6-foot forward, he wasn't a regular. He finally broke into the starting line-up as a senior. In his own words, "I was a decent high school player, nothing special."

So he paid his own way to Wisconsin-Stevens Point, a small state school, because he liked the coach, Dick Bennett. After a freshman year spent mostly on the bench, Porter emerged as a standout in his sophomore year, helping Wisconsin-Stevens Point reach the NAIA national finals, where it lost to Fort Hays State.

Porter first made a big impression on NBA scouts after his junior season, when he participated in the 1984 United States Olympic trials. In a camp stocked with blue-chippers, Porter very nearly made the team. The guards who made Coach Bobby Knight's roster included Michael Jordan, Chris Mullin, Alvin Robertson, Leon Wood, and Steve Alford. Porter, one of the four final cuts, rode to the airport with the other hopefuls who had narrowly missed out—Charles Barkley, John Stockton, and Maurice Martin.

"I thought I should have made it," Porter says now. He might have, if only he hadn't contracted chicken pox early in the trials. He was sent home for a week to recuperate, then returned at less than full strength.

Here was Porter, the guy from the school nobody had ever heard of, the guy nobody wanted out of high school,

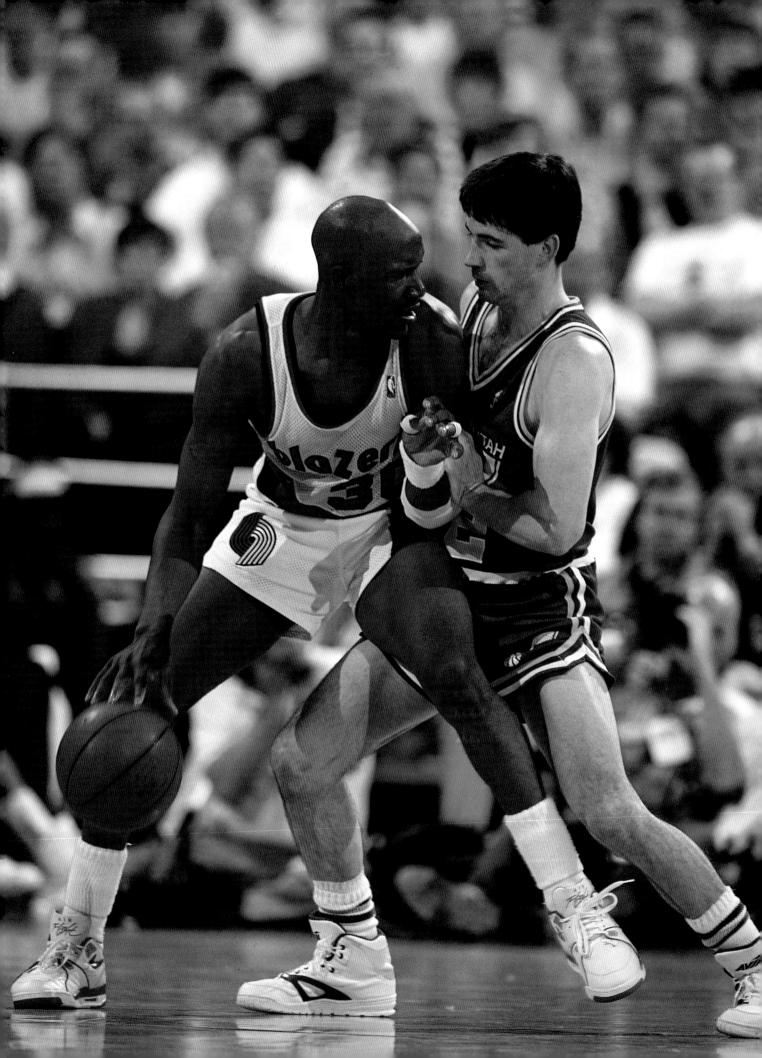

going head-to-head with some of the great names in college basketball and more than holding his own. "I really wasn't intimidated," he says. "I had enough confidence in myself, and I think it grew as the trials went on and I saw for sure that I could play with anybody. I went in trying to make sure to play my hardest and stay sound defensively. Even though I didn't make it, it was an unbelievable experience. I can't begin to explain how big it was as far as me getting known."

Aside from his physical skills, the Olympic coaches and NBA scouts liked Porter's cool head and his ability to make good decisions on the court. It's the same thing the Blazers love about him today, and he gives credit to Bennett, now a respected coach at Wisconsin-Green Bay.

"Coach Bennett did a great job of teaching me not just to play the game, but to have a feel for it," Porter explains. "I learned how important it was to be able to read situations and to be a smart player. I think I've been pretty consistent, and I think that has something to do with it." So great is Porter's respect for Bennett that he still spends a couple of weeks each summer with him, working out and preparing for the upcoming NBA season.

Terry met one other very important person in his life at Wisconsin-Stevens Point—his wife Susie. "I met her in the library through a mutual friend," Terry says. "I was a senior. She was a freshman." They were soon an item, and in August 1990 they were married.

After his senior season at Wisconsin-Stevens Point, Porter was taken by Portland as the number 24 pick in the first round of the draft. "A big surprise," he says now. "I'd talked to a lot of other clubs, but not Portland. The most important thing to me was going in the first round. Being an NAIA player, if it was the second round, I might not have gotten a chance."

Porter became the Blazers' starting point guard in his second season, the 1986-87 campaign, and quietly set about becoming one of the better players in the league at his position. He had arguably his best season in 1990-91, ranking second on the team in scoring (17.0 points) and first in assists (8.0) and steals. He was also one of the best three-point shooters in basketball and made the NBA All-Star Game for the first time, achieving his highest personal goal.

"The All-Star Game is something you dream about since you were a kid," says Porter, who took back souvenirs he will cherish forever. "The most enjoyable part of it to me was getting the opportunity to know some of the other guys on a personal basis. That's something you just don't get to do during the regular season when they're the enemy, so to speak."

When Porter came to the Blazers, he was only an average outside shooter. Gradually, he's become one of the best in the business from the perimeter, particularly in the latter stages of a tight game or in pressure situations. His teammates have taken to referring to him as Grande Huevos—"Big Eggs"—the Spanish version of "Mr. Clutch." With the game on the line, the Blazers

Terry Porter and Utah's John Stockton, two of the NBA's premier point men, have gone belly-to-belly for some brilliant individual duels over the past few seasons. ◄ Off-court, Terry's passion is golf. He shows the best simulated swing since Johnny Carson's. ▲

11

would just as soon have the ball in the hands of Porter, whether to drive and dish or take the big shot.

"I really enjoy that," he says. "You want a guy who is not afraid of having the ball in that type of situation. I like to have the ball in my hands. I don't mean to sound cocky, but I usually can make a good decision and get us a good shot. I feel very comfortable in that role."

Away from the court, Porter's interests are relatively simple. He enjoys spending time with Susie, with whom he shares another passion—golf. Terry had never tried the game until his second season in Portland. "It started just as something to do in the summertime. I played tennis the first year, but it was just too much. Golf is so relaxing and peaceful, and I enjoy the outdoors. On the golf course, you don't have a worry in the world."

Terry's other off-court interest is something he also shares with his wife—community work. All of the Blazer players devote time to worthy causes, but Porter may top the list. He was Oregon's honorary chairman for Project Graduation, encouraging high school seniors to celebrate with drug- and alcohol-free graduation parties. He helped launch Smart Moves, a program designed to reduce teenage vulnerability to gang membership, drug and alcohol use, and sexual involvement. He is a member of the board of Sixth-Man Foundation, which helps provide funds for projects to help needy children. He is active with the Boys and Girls clubs of Portland, and he is one of several players involved in buying Blazer game tickets for youths who otherwise would not have a chance to attend.

The list goes on. Perhaps most dear to his heart is the minority scholarship fund he started last year at Wisconsin-Stevens Point. He and Susie recently presented college officials with a check for $50,000.

For all these efforts, Porter was named as runner-up for the NBA's Walter Kennedy Award last season, given each year to a player for civic contributions and citizenship. "If there's a little kid in the hospital who is not doing well and loves the Blazers, many times he'll be the one to offer to visit," says Christee Sweeney, the Blazers' director of communications. "And he takes no publicity for this. Terry epitomizes the player who understands he's a role model and exercises a positive influence to the max."

"I think it's important to help where you can," says Terry. "Most guys try to give something back. It's not so much an obligation as a privilege. Kids are our future, and I want them to know they're important."

Kids are definitely in the Porters' future, Terry says. "I think we're going to have a bundle of them."

In the meantime, he isn't forgetting his roots. Next summer, he will finish his college degree at Wisconsin-Stevens Point. It has been a lot of work, but that's nothing new. "I know how hard I had to bust my tail to get to the point I am now in my career," Terry says quietly. "I think guys from small colleges work a little harder to prove themselves. I know how easily it can be gone. I won't quit working."

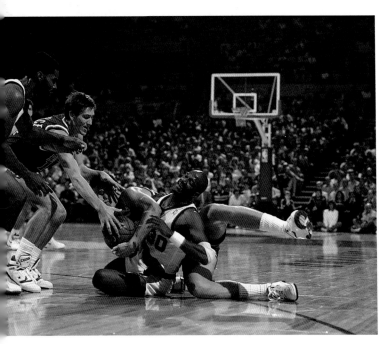

The strain of intense competition shows on Porter's face as he grapples for the ball with Phoenix's Tom Chambers. ▲ *Terry drives through the key against the Lakers' Byron Scott and Magic Johnson, preparing to dish off to an open man. Porter realized his ultimate individual goal last season when he was named to the NBA All-Star Game. At 28, in his seventh pro season, Terry has his sights set on a championship ring.* ▶

Clyde Drexler

It's Christmas in June. Boys and girls are flying up and down the basketball courts at Benson Tech, taking part in the Clyde Drexler/Sixth-Man Foundation camp. Hey, there's the man himself, towering out there in the middle.

Clyde has plenty of coaches to work with the four hundred kids, aged 8 through 17, who attend the week-long sessions. But just by being here, he gives credibility to the camp—and makes just about everyone's day.

The whistle blows, and groups of kids move from one station to the next. It's a chance to nestle up to their hero and get pointers on their game.

"Hey, Clyde," one boy says. "I got 16 points."

"It's about time," Clyde retorts. "I saw the way you played yesterday."

One small, pale boy named Clay hangs back. "Hi, Mr. Drexler," he whispers shyly. Clyde doesn't hear him, but Clay doesn't mind. Just being this close to someone this great is really something.

"Are you working on your shot?" Clyde asks a girl. "Pay attention to the coaches, work on your fundamentals, and you can really improve."

Clyde and former NBA forward Kermit Washington have joined forces to stage this free camp, which rewards students, primarily from inner-city schools, who have improved their grades, maintained perfect attendance, or shown good citizenship. Kermit puts the plan together and does the legwork. Sponsors fund the salaries for the coaches and provide shoes and shirts for the campers. Clyde provides his services free.

"This is a great opportunity for me to give something back," Clyde says. "I like the fact that the kids don't have to pay for this. They learn there are rewards for being a good student and a good citizen. One of the best things about a person in my position is I can help these kids realize they can have a life for themselves."

Clyde knows what it's like to come from a broken home, to rise up past the negative influences. His half-brother, Michael Prevost, died in a hold-up. Clyde saw the bad side of life; he chose the good—and he gives basketball credit. "It's shown me a side of life I'm not sure I'd have experienced otherwise," he says. Now kids look up to him, "Clyde The Glide," one of the game's greats.

The All-Star of today is a different man from the Clyde Drexler who came to Portland from the University of Houston as a rookie in 1983. He married Gaynell, a bright, articulate woman who may be one of the top corporate lawyers in Oregon in the years to come. He is father to two youngsters, Austin, 2, and Kathryn Elise, born in July 1991. He has gained much of the respect he didn't receive early in his career. He is more at peace with himself. And finally, he feels like an Oregonian. Clyde has made Portland his permanent home. In 1990, he and Gaynell purchased a stately, five-bedroom home tucked into a quiet corner of Portland.

As Clyde observes, "It was time. I have friends here, I play ball here, and I want to stay here full-time and enjoy living here. That's another reason I do the camp. This is

Clyde Drexler finally received his just due of national acclaim with the Blazers' success of the past two seasons. He was the subject of several articles in national publications. Here, he posed for a feature story in Inside Sports. ◄ *Clyde always tries to put his best foot forward, but for some reason, has found himself leaving a shoe behind on more than a few occasions.* ▲

15

*F*ew NBA *athletes play above the rim with the frequency of Drexler, here slicing for two points between a pair of Minnesota defenders.* ▲ *There's no player who more closely approximates the considerable skills of Michael Jordan than Drexler, here preparing to drive against Jordan's body-hugging defense. Michael is the Prince of Air, but Clyde can glide with the best of them.* ▶

where you work, where you live, where your kids grow up. Anything I can do for the community to make it a better place to live, I'd like to try to do."

It's safe to say Drexler is the most popular Trail Blazer of all time, and he's probably the most recognizable figure in the state. He can't walk a city block without drawing a "Hey Clyde!" or "Hello, Mr. Drexler." He is unfailingly polite although admittedly a little embarrassed by all the fuss. When an employee of a local golf course tells him he raises the property values by playing, he smiles and thanks him. Afterward, he can only shake his head.

"I'm used to this kind of thing," he says, "but sometimes it just amazes you. I feel like it's an honor. They obviously respect your talents, but I also think people know I'm a nice person. Otherwise, they wouldn't have so much enthusiasm when they see me."

Clyde understands autograph seekers better than most pro athletes, because he was one himself. He lived ten minutes from the Houston Astrodome as a kid and got autographs from major-leaguers all the time. "I went to every home game of the Astros," he says. "Fifty cents got you into the center-field upper bleachers."

Clyde was born in New Orleans but moved with his mother, Eunice Scott, to Houston when he was three. His father, James Drexler, a mill worker when Clyde was a child, still lives in New Orleans, but he long ago ceased to be a factor in Clyde's life. "He'd send me a card maybe once a year, for my birthday or Christmas, but you never really thought much about it because you didn't know any better," Clyde says. "I wish he'd kept in better contact with his kids, but he did the best he could."

It was Eunice who did most of the work raising her seven children. "She was both mother and father to us," Clyde says. "She did a super job. I have a tremendous amount of respect for her. She's opinionated, but she had to be. She did everything it took to raise her kids and make sure she provided well for them."

The family lived in a three-bedroom brick home in a lower-middle class, blue-collar neighborhood. Eunice worked in a grocery store, a fact Clyde recalls with appreciation. "We never went home hungry. We didn't have much money, but it wasn't that bad. We were very close. We knew everybody in the neighborhood. The schools were close by. I wouldn't change it for the world."

With a job to fulfill and so many children to look after in what was primarily a one-parent household, Eunice left her kids on their own a lot. "She gave us a lot of freedom," Clyde says. "She expected you to behave and take care of your responsibilities."

Most of her kids did that. The oldest son, Michael Prevost, strayed, and it cost him his life. Michael, who was eight years older than his half-brother, Clyde, got involved with drugs. "He'd come home, all doped up, creating havoc around the house," Clyde remembers. The other kids would wonder, 'What's wrong with him?' As a kid, you're aware of all that stuff. I used to try to help

him. He was the kind of guy who was always in trouble. He'd get kicked out of school. It was too bad."

When Prevost was 18, he was killed by a policeman while attempting to rob a pharmacy. "It was the worst feeling," Clyde says. "I was devastated. I don't think my mother ever recovered. She blamed herself."

Clyde loved all sports as a kid, particularly football— he was an Oilers fan—but he was not an instant success as an athlete. "I was horrible at first," he says. "I was the slowest guy on the block for many years."

In junior high, things changed. He grew four or five inches in one year, took up karate, and lifted weights. Suddenly, the coordination was there. Even so, he was not a star on his ninth-grade team. "I was like 13th man, and we only had 12 uniforms. Sometimes I didn't get to travel, because we didn't have enough uniforms, but I was just happy to be on the team."

As a 6-2 sophomore at Ross Sterling High School, Clyde says he turned out a day late and was booted out by Coach Clifford Jackson. "I didn't want to go out to begin with," Clyde recalls, "so I was late the second day of practice, and the coach said, 'Give me 25 push-ups.' I couldn't do them, and he said, 'Get out of my gym.'"

Then Jackson saw him playing at noon one day and asked him to turn out the following season. Clyde refused. "I told him, 'You didn't give me a chance.' But that afternoon when I got home, he was there talking to my mom. She made me play." From that point on, Clyde devoted himself to basketball.

"I became a gym rat," he says. "I had a key to the gym—I got it from the janitor—and I shot a lot by myself, or with Michael Young. If I didn't have the keys, he did. He played in the same district, but at another school. He was the best player in the state. I played 24/7—24 hours a day, 7 days a week. I shot, lifted weights, jumped rope, and did calisthenics. I became a fanatic. I had a goal to one day be the best." His heroes were Julius Erving and Walt Frazier.

Clyde first dunked a volleyball at age 14. In high school, he was a good leaper, but not a great one. "I was an OK dunker, but everybody could do the things I was doing," he says. "Matter of fact, we had a better dunker on our team. Actually, I was kind of meek."

Clyde became a starter as a junior and, as a 6-6 senior, was captain and an all-city selection. But even then, he wasn't a sensation. "I wasn't all-state," he says. "I wasn't even among the top ten guys in the state."

He visited New Mexico State and Texas Tech before deciding to stay home and play for Houston's Guy Lewis. It was a good decision. He became an All-American and renowned member of "Phi Slamma Jamma," helping the Cougars twice to the NCAA final four. He became known as "The Glide," a flamboyant dunker and tremendous all-around talent, the first Cougar to total 1,000 points, 900 rebounds, and 300 assists.

"I wouldn't trade my years at Houston," he says. "I blossomed as a player and as a person. The school's

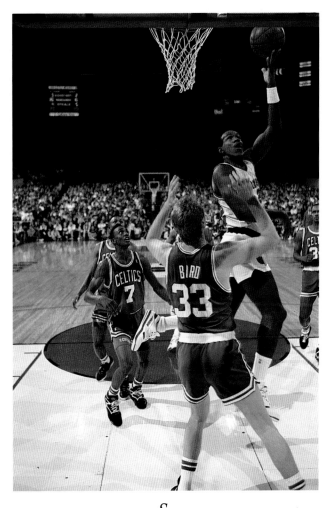

Say what you want about Drexler's other talents; just don't forget his dunking ability. He sends one spinning through twine on the San Antonio Spurs. "I don't go into a dunk with a plan," Clyde says. "I usually react to a situation. I'm often just as surprised with the result as the next guy." ◄ Drexler scores with either hand, as shown against Larry Bird of the Boston Celtics. ▲

19

atmosphere was conducive to the type of person I was and am, and Guy's program was super, really laid-back."

Clyde left college a year early to be available for the draft. When Portland made him the 14th pick in the first round, he wasn't exactly turning cartwheels. "I was disappointed," he admits. "I thought Houston was going to take me with the third pick. That's the reason I came out of college. Then the Rockets took Rodney McCray."

It was a frustrating time for Drexler, who was unaccustomed to spending much time on the bench. The move from Houston to Portland left him crying culture shock, and Jack Ramsay wasn't an easy coach to break into the NBA with. Clyde averaged about 15 minutes and 7.7 points off the bench during his rookie season, spelling Jim Paxson at off guard and Calvin Natt at small forward. "There was no spot for me," he says now, "but I felt I could have contributed more, gotten a little more time."

The Blazers won 48 games during the 1983-84 season. "We had a pretty good team," Clyde says. "But were we happy with 48? Why not 60?" Clyde wanted to be traded. "I must have asked to be traded twenty times before, during, and after my first season," he says. "I learned a lot from watching Jimmy, but I wanted to go to a place where a team would use me. At one point, I couldn't even get any time in practice. Jeff Lamp was ahead of me at the two-guard. Jack Ramsay never knew if I could play or not. I respected Jack. He taught me a lot about the game, but I just wanted to play."

Clyde was miffed when the Blazers selected off guard/small forward Bernard Thompson in the first round of the 1984 draft. "That shows you how much confidence they had in me," he says. But Clyde got his break when Paxson held out at the season's start, and he was able to show his stuff. He spent most of the year as the team's sixth man, averaging 17.7 points while getting major minutes at the two and three spots. The next season, he became a starter and played in his first All-Star Game.

Drexler still had one more major storm to weather as a Blazer. The Blazers were productive when Mike Schuler replaced Ramsay as head coach for the 1986-87 season. They won 49 games during the regular season, and Clyde had a big year, averaging 21.7 points. But coach and star didn't see eye to eye. Schuler's problems with Clyde had at least something to do with the coach's dismissal midway through the 1988-89 campaign.

An anonymous coach—Schuler, presumably—said, "It's not that Clyde is not a nice guy. He is a nice guy. He's one of those guys who carries a switchblade in his back pocket. He's late all the time. He doesn't work hard enough in practice. . . . He's always complaining to the front office—all those things that can hurt a team a thousand ways, especially if he's your star. . . . He always seemed to be one of those guys who thought it was more important to be cool than anything else. What . . . kind of 'star' is that?"

"It sounds like a coach who has been fired and who is blaming other people for his failure," Clyde told Roy

*L*ike a lot of folks, Michael Jordan is a Clyde Drexler fan, but Clyde has learned there is a price to his fame. "I'm one of those guys who signs autographs almost every night after games, but there are times when it would be nice to be left alone. I'd love to take my wife and kids to the Rose Festival, for instance, but there's no way I can do that and enjoy myself." ▲ Drexler defends Magic Johnson well, and one of Clyde's goals is to make the NBA's All-Defensive team: "Michael never made it until he started talking about it," Clyde says. ▶

Firestone on his "Up Close" television show. "When the team had a good year, not a thing was said. When we had trouble, that's when all the stuff came out."

Clyde believes the whole thing was blown out of proportion to make somebody a scapegoat. As he observes, "I'm the kind of guy who is not going to let you make me a scapegoat without telling you what I think."

Schuler's successor, Rick Adelman, came to the Blazers as an assistant coach in Drexler's rookie year. They have grown together. Clyde trusts Adelman, and the two get along famously. Clyde works harder in practice—yes, he's not the best practice player in NBA history—and is quick to give credit to Rick for the team's success.

Under Adelman, Clyde became a team leader and sacrificed some of his scoring average to help the team in other areas. Without his contributions, the Blazers would not have reached the Western Conference Finals two straight seasons and played in the NBA Finals in 1990.

"You always should focus on how to fit your skills into the team concept and do what you can to help the team win," The Glide says. "Early in my career, they needed my scoring. The last two years we've had more help in that department, so I've tried to do other things. I think I've played good defense for many years, but I've never made an All-Defensive team. My reputation as a dunker and flashy offensive player has a lot to do with that, I think. The voters consider you a dunker and think you can't do both."

No getting around it, though. When the name "Clyde Drexler" comes up, the word "dunk" comes down. He's had some of the most spectacular slams in history. His 43-inch vertical reach is one reason, but springs aren't everything. "You have to let your instincts take over," Clyde says. "You take advantage of what the defense gives you. I don't go into a dunk with a plan. I usually react to a situation. I'm often just as surprised as the next guy."

Drexler's personal life is in crisp order. He met Gaynell through mutual friends while she was practicing corporate law in Manhattan in 1987, and they were married in 1988. "She has so many nice qualities that I was really impressed. She's intellectual, sincere, a warm person above anything else. Marriage has been great and having kids has been great. The little things we overlook in life add up, and I've really been blessed."

Today, Clyde is a five-time NBA All-Star and the leading scorer in Trail Blazer history. He signed a contract extension in 1990 that calls for him to make a record $8 million during the 1995-96 season, when he will be 33. There is only one little matter left: he has never won a national title in the NCAA or NBA. Will he ever win one?

"I'm an extreme optimist," Clyde responds. "I'm a guy who is going to win it. We have the team to win an NBA title for years to come. This organization has done a super job putting together a group of guys who are great players, unselfish players, guys who want to win. Yes, I think we'll win. But even if we don't, I think I can live with myself. I've had a pretty good career."

The game highlights three of its brightest stars: Clyde Drexler extends for lay-up between the Lakers' James Worthy and Magic Johnson. ◄ *Plenty is on the line during the play-offs, and an occasional difference of opinion arises. Jerome Kersey heats up in an argument with referee Jack Nies as Williams and Porter listen in.* ▲

Buck Williams

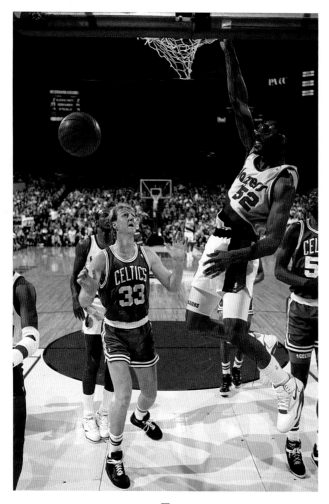

Fly away, Bird Man: Williams jams against the Celtics. ▲ *A promotional photo for a charitable cause, with a rickety basket as its backdrop, brought back memories for Buck of his childhood in Rocky Mount, North Carolina. He became one of the game's most respected players, and credits John Lucas and Len Elmore, two players who preceded him at the University of Maryland, as role models. "They'd come back to Maryland after the season and they were always down to earth. I felt a professional athlete should carry himself like that."* ▶

It's grand-opening day at Wilsonville Thriftway, and the grocery store located twenty minutes south of Portland, along Interstate 5, may never again reach this level of excitement. Hot dogs and soda pop are on sale at give-away prices, balloons are going gratis, but the draw is a chance to get a free autograph from Buck Williams.

Blazer fans young and old have waited in line for as long as five hours to get a signature and an up-close look at their hero. And for two hours, with the heat of a 90-degree summer day bearing down, the veteran power forward of the Trail Blazers sits at a table and signs hundreds of autographs on pictures, posters, pennants, shirts, shorts, shoes, books, basketballs, hats, casts, cards, schedule cards, and autograph books.

Rob Heroux, a season-ticket holder in a motorized wheelchair, waits an hour and a half for his autograph. "I like his Christian witness," says Heroux, who has multiple sclerosis. "He's an outstanding example to the community. Both my wife and I really appreciate him."

Paul Chase, 19, has come all the way from Aloha to get a poster signed by his all-time favorite player. "I like him because he's a team player," Chase says. "He does all the dirty work. He's not a showboat. He doesn't take drugs. He's a family man."

Jenny Troyer, 11, has pictures of Blazers hung all over her room. She has Buck sign her diary book. On the top of it, she has written: "Today I'm going to see Buck Williams. Isn't that cool? I'm so excited."

All sorts of people drop by. "Any good fishing lately, Buck?" one man asks. "Went out twice and came home empty-handed both times," Buck answers, laughing. An old man wonders, "Do you suppose his arm will recover by next season?" as the bionic arm continues to pump out autographs. An elderly woman asks, "Do you sign for grandmas, too?" Buck winks, "That's my first priority."

A few minutes before the autograph session closes, a man pleads with Pepsi's sales and marketing manager, Scott Gray. "My wife just had a baby. She's a big Buck Williams fan. I'm on my way to the hospital right now. Is there any way I can get a ball signed?" He leaves with an autograph and an "A" for ingenuity.

Buck and Clyde Drexler, perhaps the Blazers' two biggest stars, are among the best at handling fans, although they occasionally draw the line when they are with their families. "Clyde and I are similar," Buck says. "We never feel as though we've reached the point of stardom where we can't be ourselves and make ourselves visible to the community. We understand how important it is, especially in a city like Portland."

Since coming to Portland from New Jersey for the 1989-90 season, Williams became something of a living legend. The Blazers, 39-43 the season before he arrived, advanced to NBA Finals his first year, and he was given credit for adding toughness to a team critics called soft. He backed down to no one. He was the missing link.

Buck and his wife, Mimi, had apprehensions about living in Portland, but these quickly dissolved. With a

Basketball is important but it's not the only thing for Williams and Duckworth, who enjoy the salmon fishing opportunities of the Northwest. ▲ *Buck has worn protective goggles since sustaining a scratch to an eyeball in the 1990 play-off series against Dallas.* ▶

lovely house not far from the Lewis & Clark College campus, the Williamses and their 2-year-old son, Julien, now call Portland home.

"After experiencing eight years in New Jersey, I can fully appreciate Portland," Buck says. "The quality of life out here is a lot better than on the East Coast. I was really concerned about the racial imbalance when I came out here, but it's a lot better for African-Americans out here than back East. And it's been a phenomenal experience to play on a team with exceptional players and coaches in a community that supports a team like this."

More than any of the team, Williams has come a long way, and he firmly says, "My background and my heritage is where I draw my strength." Buck grew up in a four-room house in Rocky Mount, North Carolina, youngest of six children born to Moses and Betty Williams. His given name was Charles Linwood Williams, but when he was 12, a friend of his father said, "That big Buck is ready to go hunting right now," and the tag stuck.

Buck's grandparents on both sides were sharecroppers, picking tobacco and cotton. His parents worked in the cotton fields during Buck's childhood, until Moses moved to highway construction. "A lot of times, they were short-changed by white landowners," Buck says, "but they survived and carved quite a niche for themselves."

Buck feels so strongly about his ancestors that he became a voracious student of genealogy, spending many hours digging through the state archives in Raleigh. He traced his family back to 1795 on the maternal side. "I was fascinated to see the slaveowners' inventories," he says. "It took me down a lot of roads."

Buck's father completed the third grade; his mother, the sixth. "I think my parents, considering their schooling, have maxed out their potential," he says. "I'm very respectful of them having the fortitude they've had."

Buck describes his father as a "quiet, personable, friendly type of person. He'd give his last coin to a friend. It made me sort of angry at him at times, but that's his personality." Buck bought his parents a new house when he joined the NBA, but Moses still spends time at the old one, refusing to sell it or tear it down.

"I resented my dad for many years because he spent so much time away from home working," Buck says. "But over the last four or five years I've begun to understand things. The poet Robert Bly wrote that when you're young and growing up, the son and mother are like a conspiracy against the father, and I think that's true to an extent. Now I've begun to understand why he had to be out of the house, and it's made us much closer."

Buck's mother is ill with kidney disease and has to be dialyzed every other day. Buck, who remembers her as "a vibrant, fun-loving, high-spirited person," finds it hard to accept. "That's part of aging," he says, "but it's hard to accept that in your mother. My mother and I have always been close. She was the heart and soul of the family because my father spent so much time working. She always sort of meshed with the kids' activities. I remember

days when she'd have one or two dollars in her pocket and she'd spend it on us. She was willing to give anything for us every day. That's what love is all about."

Buck's oldest brother was raised by his maternal grandparents, but the other siblings grew up with Buck in the family's humble abode, which for many years was without indoor plumbing. "We were poor," Buck recalls, "but I don't recall ever being hungry. The Williamses were not afraid of hard work. My friends wanted to borrow money from me because, from the time I was 12, I always had a job."

Betty Williams was a religious person. Her family attended Saint James Baptist Church and always lived by Christian virtues. "When the man gave me too much change at the grocery store, I always gave it back," says Buck. "My parents gave me values."

As a youngster, Buck loved the outdoors. A creek not far from his home was a favorite spot. He and his friends would put nails and string on two-by-four blocks and catch tadpoles. "A biological experience," he says.

When Buck was 12, Moses, Jr., his 16-year-old brother, drowned while swimming in a pond. It was a traumatic experience for Buck, who was closer to Moses than to his other brothers and sisters, but Buck responded with an inner toughness. "I recall sitting in church at his funeral, and I looked at my father and, for some reason, I couldn't cry. I don't know if it was masochism or what. Even though I missed him dearly . . . I never cried."

Buck had a two-sided personality as a youngster. Shy, perhaps lacking in self-confidence, he rarely spoke in school. Outside school, "My friends and I were like the Three Stooges. We carried on and fooled around. I was like that until I stepped onto my porch at home. That's where it ceased, because my mother wouldn't tolerate it."

Though football was his first love, basketball soon replaced it. A friend who lived behind their home had a basket, and Buck shot there and at the playground for hours. By the time he was a 6-3 ninth-grader, he was dunking the ball. It helped him to get out of his shell at school. "The first organized game I played, the coach called a play for me, and I scored. After that, my friends always kidded me and said that's when I started talking."

About that time, Buck took his first out-of-state trip to participate in the renowned Sonny Hill Summer League in Philadelphia. It was his first exposure to big-time ball, and he was motivated. Then, in his junior year, Rocky Mount High got a new coach. Reggie Henderson transformed Buck's game, making him focus on his strengths, teaching him the fundamentals.

He became obsessed with the game. "I enjoyed it because it was something I felt I could master. Later on, I saw it as a chance to advance my position in life."

As a 6-6, 180-pound senior, Buck led Rocky Mount to the state 4-A title, averaging 20 points and 20 rebounds during the tournament. Scouts were calling him, but he decided on Maryland. Coach Lefty Driesell, a down-home type of guy, won him over with a recruiting visit.

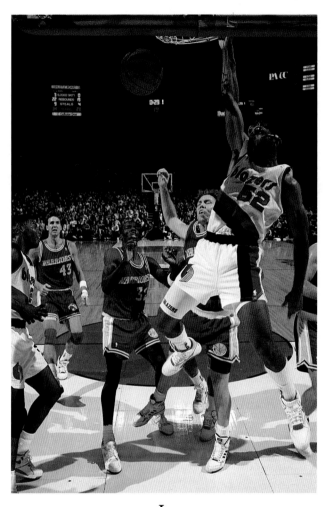

If there's a single element Buck has added to the Blazers, it's toughness on defense, which he displays in blocking a shot against Golden State. ◄ *Buck was a member of the NBA's All-Defensive first team last season. He can also run the court and is a great finisher at the end of a fast break. Here, he slams on the Warriors.* ▲

29

"Lefty was very comfortable coming down to our poor little house and having a relationship with my family. He had no problems with black-eyed peas or cornbread or whatever. We saw him as sincere."

Buck played three years at Maryland before entering the draft after his junior year, when he was taken as number two pick by New Jersey. He knew he would be chosen quickly, and his family needed the money. The first thing he did after signing a contract was to buy his parents a new house.

In 1988, Buck returned to Maryland to get his degree. "I've faced a lot of challenges in my life," he observes. "One was trying to shake the dumb-jock stereotype. Getting your degree sets that aside. I feel sort of liberated." He says his mother was prouder of him when he earned his diploma than when he signed his first pro pact.

During his freshman year at Maryland, Buck met Mimi. "I was working out in Cole Fieldhouse when I glanced up and saw this gorgeous young lady. I sent a ballboy up to get a phone number." They were married in 1985.

Today they are parents, and Julien keeps the Buckster hopping. "What a unique experience, to be a father," Buck marvels. "It has really changed me as a person. It forces you to be more unselfish, to be a protector. I see so much of myself in my son. I take him down to the park and find myself sliding down the slide more than him. Of course, he wants to shoot hoops on his little basket all day long."

Williams had a great career during his eight seasons in New Jersey, making the All-Star Team three times, proving himself a top rebounder and inside defender. The only thing missing was winning. The Nets won only one play-off series, and when he was traded to Portland, Buck wondered if he'd ever play with a championship contender. That dream has been realized. Today there is no doubt in his mind: the Blazers can and will win big.

Buck's obsessions run in cycles. These include piano ("I'm OK"), genealogy, woodworking, financial planning, video games, and a long-lasting hobby—building radio-controlled model planes. He has built nine. "The thought of reading blueprints, building something with my hands, and then taking it out into the field and seeing whether or not it'll fly . . . it's a great challenge."

Buck loves a good cause. He has served as honorary chairman for such charities as March of Dimes and the Emanuel Hospital Children's Gala, is a spokesman for the NBA for prevention of child abuse, and sits on the board of directors for the House of Umoja, a project to steer inner-city youths out of gangs and into education.

He remains a Christian and has delivered occasional talks at churches in the Portland area. "My religious background has served me well all my life," Buck says. "The Lord has blessed me and made me realize I am an example in the community. Being a Christian keeps you focused on doing the right thing. That's the ultimate witness, the way I live my life."

It's pow-wow time for the Trail Blazers, who believe that communication and camaraderie have been the keys to the development of a oneness of purpose. Coach Rick Adelman and his assistants, John Wetzel and Jack Schalow, have given the players plenty of leeway in making their own decisions, and the majority of the time those decisions have been good ones. ▲ A bird's-eye angle catches the Blazers in unison inside the paint. ▶

Jerome Kersey

Jerome Kersey is tickled and fretting at the same time. He has just bought his grandparents, Herman and Elizabeth Kersey, a brand-new Mercedes-Benz 525. "Got to sell one of my cars to do it," he says, winking. "Love those cars. They're like my kids right now."

Jerome is more than willing to part with one of his "kids" for his grandparents. In his mind, they *are* his parents. His mother, Dolores Florence, gave birth to him out of wedlock when she was 18 years old, and his grandparents raised him. He has always called his mother "Dolores" and his grandparents "Mom and Dad."

Shortly after he signed his first contract with the Portland Trail Blazers in 1984, Jerome had placed a down payment on a new home for his grandparents in Clarksville, Virginia, the town where he grew up. It's a modest three-bedroom home in a quiet area on the outskirts of town. "They didn't want anything elaborate," he says.

The Kerseys were knocked out when they flew west to see the five-bedroom, 6,000-square-foot Portland home their grandson purchased in 1990. It's a beautiful, two-story house with an immaculately landscaped yard, a pool and hot tub, and a back-yard view of the city that stretches for miles and miles. "All they could say was, 'This house is so big.' My grandfather was here two or three days, and he was ready to leave. I said, 'What you gotta do?' He said, 'Nothing, I just gotta get back.' It was too much for him. He wanted to get back to his comfort zone. I think next time she'll come out here by herself and stay for a couple of weeks."

Jerome bought them a Volkswagen early in his career. Then he decided they needed something a little nicer. When he brought the Mercedes home to Clarksville, his grandmother didn't say much. "She just looked at it, and my grandfather looked at it. But my grandfather said, after I left, she cried."

It's a thrill for Jerome to make Herman, 68, and Elizabeth, 65, happy. He figures he can never repay them for raising him.

At 29, Jerome Kersey is starting forward for the Trail Blazers, one of the best teams in basketball. He recently signed a contract extension that will give him an average of $3.7 million annually over four years, ending with the 1995-96 season. His contract has given him financial stability and the chance to make sure his grandparents have that, too.

As a child, Jerome never knew his father, and he regarded his mother as "just like one of my aunts." Herman and Elizabeth, who had six children of their own, took Jerome in and made him one of their sons in their always-too-small house in a rural section of Clarksville, a town of ten thousand. Both grandparents held blue-collar jobs. Herman worked at a sawmill; Elizabeth, at a wool and cloth company, then at a candy factory. His aunts and uncles, who seemed like older siblings to Jerome, often had jobs, too. There wasn't a

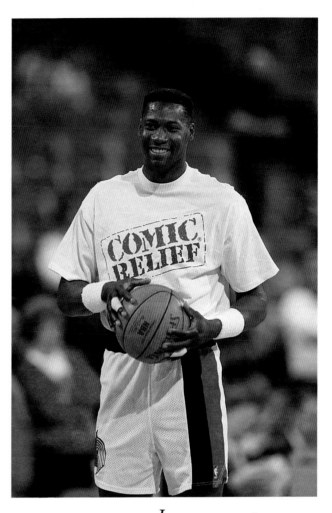

Jerome Kersey's future is so bright, he has to wear shades. ◄ *Kersey is a fun-loving guy who is enjoying his single status for now but figures he'll get married toward the end of his NBA career. Women haven't always been a priority in his life. "In high school, I was into sports," he says. "I didn't date any girls. I'd much rather play basketball than be around some girl."* ▲

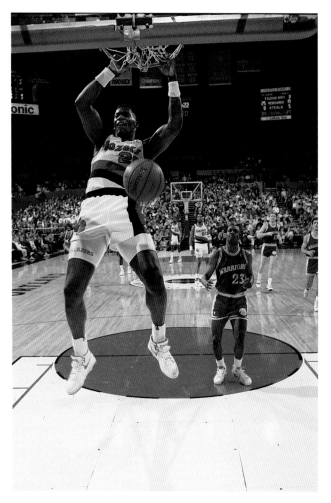

Renowned as one of the most exciting dunkers, Kersey's thunder slam shakes the rafters in the Coliseum in a game against Golden State. ▲ *Do real men wear black? Just ask bad dudes Kersey, Duckworth, and Williams, who are posing for a promotional poster in threads that would do the Los Angeles Raiders proud.* ▶

whole lot of money coming in, but the family got by fine. And there was always an abundance of love.

"Herman is a real quiet guy," Jerome says. "He pretends he can't hear sometimes. Then you'll be whispering something, and he'll hear loud and clear. I'm close to him in some ways. He doesn't get close to a lot of people—even his own kids. You know he loves you, but he won't let it come across too often."

Elizabeth is very warm. "She stays cheerful all the time. She taught me a lot of things about life. She'd always give me her last dime. She's my heart and soul. I love her more than anyone in the world." Jerome credits his upbringing with helping him to keep perspective on life. "A lot of the guys," he says, "didn't have fathers around to guide them."

Jerome's father didn't enter the picture until about three years ago, when he showed up for a Blazer game with the Washington Bullets at Landover, Maryland. "It was like meeting a stranger," Jerome says. "When we're on the East Coast he comes to games and we talk, but I guess I'm apprehensive. I'll never forget the time he came to Clarksville when I was a kid. He came one block from where I was staying—and he knew I was there—but he didn't come by. From that point on, I just felt it didn't matter anymore."

As a youngster, Jerome loved the freedom of the wide-open spaces around Clarksville. For a time he spent summers in nearby Richmond with his mother, but he didn't like the city. "You couldn't roam when you wanted to. I found it very confining." What he liked to do was go to Bug Island Lake to fish with his great-grandmother. "It was an everyday thing I looked forward to. Catfish, crappie, bass. I'd fish in the morning and play basketball the rest of the day."

Jerome says he stayed out of trouble except for a running battle with his cousin, Clifton Kersey, Jr. "We used to fight every day," he grins. "It turned into a ritual. We used to fight just looking at each other. We'd say, 'Hey, we haven't fought yet today,' and we'd go at it."

The population of Clarksville was divided fairly evenly between the whites and the blacks. Although Kersey didn't feel much overt racism, he believes there were undercurrents. "A lot of blacks and whites didn't interact. I think they do more so now, but it's still there. We're talking about southern Virginia. There are certain things you have to watch around town. There's still a little bit of tension."

Jerome's roughneck lifestyle made football his first love, but football took a backseat to basketball as he entered Bluestone High School. "There were a lot of guys who were better athletes than me," he notes, "but they let some of the social things hold them back—alcohol, maybe, or just plain lack of motivation. I was into sports. I didn't date any girls. I'd much rather play basketball than be around some girl."

By his junior year, Kersey was a 6-3, 190-pound starting point guard. When all the big guys graduated, he

played center, averaging 18 points and eight rebounds. But there wasn't a huge market among major colleges for 6-3 centers, and Kersey wound up at Division II Longwood College in Virginia.

He turned into the recruiting bonanza of a career for Coach Cal Luther, who couldn't believe it when Kersey showed up at school in the fall, standing 6-6. "It was like, 'You're not the Jerome Kersey I recruited,'" Kersey laughs.

By the end of his freshman season, Kersey was 215 and throwing his body around with the reckless abandon that is his signature in the NBA. "I've always figured if you can't play 110 percent, there's no use playing," Kersey says. "I'm not afraid of getting hurt. When you play not to get hurt, that's when you get hurt. A lot of guys have the skills, but who is going to be the guy out there running down loose balls and diving on the floor? I always admired guys who played like that, guys like Dave Cowens. A lot of guys won't work hard every play. I figured I'd work harder than the next guy. I said that was what would separate me from the rest of the players."

Kersey believes a drill Luther used in practice, called "Put a lid on it," helped him with his ambition. "You'd have to cross half court on every fast-break situation or he'd make you run sprints," Jerome says. "I've gotten a lot of hustle baskets just because I think about that."

Portland made him the final pick of the second round in the 1984 draft, and Jerome beat out Jack Ramsay favorite Pete Verhoeven for the last forward spot on the roster. When Kiki Vandeweghe was hurt during the 1987-88 season, Kersey moved into the starting lineup and has been there ever since.

Kersey has a radiant smile and has become one of the most popular of the Blazer players, not only for his never-say-die style of play and remarkable dunking ability but also for his likable demeanor. He is normally cooperative with the media, though he lapsed during the 1991 play-offs, refusing to talk after a couple of difficult losses.

"I was down and just got carried away," he says. "It was a mistake."

He is good with the public but believes the crush can get to be too much. "I like our fans," he says, "and I like the attention. It's very enjoyable. I shake people's hands all day, but there are times when autographs get to be too hectic. I've been out to nightclubs with friends and had women get offended when I didn't sign. 'Why are you out, then,' they ask. 'Why aren't you home?' Sometimes, people think there is no other part of you than basketball. It's funny. I've been washing my car, and people come by and say, 'You do that yourself?' I've had people ask, 'You don't drive that car by yourself, do you?'"

Consequently, people sometimes think he's arrogant, Kersey says. He admits he can be standoffish. "I don't let people just come up and talk to me. I may start looking around or go talk to somebody I know. You

*A*nother Kersey jam session, this one against Seattle. Jerome is one of the league's most athletic players, but he didn't really develop until he went to college. "In high school, there were a lot of guys who were better athletes than me," he says, "but they let some of the social things hold them back—alcohol, maybe, or just plain lack of motivation." ◄ Always one to stand up for a cause, Kersey has a lively discussion with Magic Johnson in Game One of the 1991 Western Conference Finals. ▲

37

can't let everybody be your friend, and it gets tiresome to talk shop all the time."

As much as any other player on the Portland Trail Blazers, Kersey enjoys clowning around with his friends and teammates. He loves to pick up and hug babies and to be playful with children. He likes to party and have a good time.

He is single, and he likes to have fun. "I like to be silly sometimes and not have people look at you real funny. The people who really know me know that side of me. I'm a big kid at heart. I still feel like I'm 21 or 22, even less than that sometimes. I have to catch myself—hey, I'm almost 30—but that's the fun part of it. If you think like that, you're going to always be young.

"I like a lot of music and going to clubs, but I don't dance. I'm a people-watcher. I like to relax, kick back, have a few cold Heinekens. People say, 'They let you guys drink?' We're responsible adults. We know what we have to do."

Because of who he is and what he does, people are always going to scrutinize Kersey. "Some people act like we're gods, that we shouldn't do anything wrong. That's not the way it is. I have to live my own life by my own rules and standards. I have to say that to myself sometimes. I can't let somebody else run my life. If I make a mistake, it's my own mistake."

If his lifestyle is fast, so are his cars. Currently, he has a 1986 Mercedes 500 SL, a 1989 Porsche 911, and a 1989 BMW 750. "I'm a car enthusiast," Jerome remarks in an understatement. "Cars are kind of an extension of your personality. They get your blood boiling."

Six players on the current roster—Clyde Drexler, Buck Williams, Terry Porter, Kevin Duckworth, Danny Ainge, and Walter Davis—have played in the NBA All-Star Game. Kersey is the only starter not to have made it. He prides himself on being a team player, but still, it hurts. "The thing that was very disappointing," he says, "was when I wasn't even on the All-Star ballot two years ago. That was kind of disheartening."

Kersey believes he has had a good career in Portland so far. "I've progressed each year and bettered a skill from the year before. I've established myself as one of the better players at my position. I go out and work hard every night. Pretty soon I know I'm going to make the All-Star Game. If I don't, well, I'll know I played as hard as I could."

That, Kersey feels, would be a nice epitaph on his tombstone. The man who always gave his all. "It'd be great to feel I could be an example for a young kid to follow. For me, it was Dr. J. I wanted to be as good as the guy. The adulation I had for him . . . well, I'd like to leave that for some kid.

"Pro athletes set examples, and I think I set a good example on the court. If a kid watches me and says, 'Hey, I like the way Jerome Kersey plays, I want to be like him,' that'd be a good way to look back on my career."

An active body like Kersey's needs a breather at times. ▲ Coach Rick Adelman has earned respect with his peerless bench work since taking over midway through the 1988-89 season. Adelman, the first team captain of the Trail Blazers (1971-72) and later assistant coach for the team for six years, is an excellent communicator and motivator and clearly is one of the keen minds in the game. ▶ Blazer basketball has experienced a wave of success over the past two seasons. ▶ ▶

Kevin Duckworth

Six hundred-plus elementary students have been looking forward to this moment for months. They could not be more thrilled if Janet Jackson, Bart Simpson, and the Teenage Mutant Ninja Turtles were all putting in a personal appearance. The William Walker Auditorium is electric with anticipation.

When Kevin Duckworth moved into the house directly across the street from the Beaverton school, the students adopted the Trail Blazers' 7-foot, 275-pound center as one of their own. "In Duck We Trust," reads a huge banner running across the front of the school.

Suddenly, a hush comes over the building. Just as suddenly, a roar that must have shaken structures from Forest Grove to Gresham erupts. The Duck has arrived! He strides through a doorway and into the auditorium. He looks a bit embarrassed as he strides slowly to the podium to a thunderous ovation, smiling, nodding his head shyly. Some of the kids in the audience look up at his massive figure with awe. Others giggle. Some scream with delight. Some wave banners they have prepared.

"This is great," Duckworth tells the group after the craziness has subsided. "It's an honor to be here, and it's an honor to live by your school. You kids are great. You treat me with respect. I'd like to say hello to the ladies who walk by my house every morning at 8:30 and say, 'Good morning, Mr. Duckworth.' I do hear you. I'd just like to say thank you for having me here. It's great to have your support."

After students perform a pair of rap dance numbers on stage, the kids pose some interesting questions, and the Duck offers some revealing responses.

Who is your hero? "It'd probably be my father. He taught me a lot growing up."

If you could choose another occupation in life, what would it be? "I believe I'd be a construction worker. I did it in college and while I was growing up, and I like doing things with my hands."

What are the best and worst things about being a pro athlete? "The best thing is having people recognize your accomplishments. The hardest thing is to understand why you get so much attention. There are a lot of times you don't want it, but you get it anyway."

What do you like about your Blazer teammates? "They are great guys. I've never been around a bunch of greater guys in my life. Everyone's nice. Sometimes they're moody, but they're a bunch of great people."

Tell us about Blazer One (the team's leased jet). "It seats all us big guys. It's not all cramped up. We have two flight attendants, who serve us whatever food we want to eat. It's not like airplane food—it's home food."

Who is your idol? "Darryl Dawkins."

What is your favorite number? "Double zero."

How did you get so big? "Ask my parents."

Why are your dogs named after cars? "Mercedes was named after a friend of mine, and when I got my next dog, I figured I better name it Benz. Then I named the next one Porsche."

When Kevin was a kid, he shot baskets in his backyard 'til the rooster crowed. He still likes to put up shots, two or three at a time if possible. ◄ This isn't Kevin's latest Halloween costume. It's another way of showing the "Double Zero" he wears on his jersey. ▲

43

Who Is your best friend? "Clyde Drexler."

Why are you so big? "Why are you so small?"

When is your birthday? "If you laugh, I'm not going to tell you — April Fool's Day."

Don't you shoot three-pointers? "No, it keeps me out of trouble."

What size shoe do you wear? "A 10. You don't believe me? It's a 15."

Do you consider yourself a celebrity? "To be honest, I don't. The only place I feel I'm known very well is here in Oregon. I can go other places in the States and get recognized, but not like here."

Later, Duckworth admits he is touched. "It makes such an impact on you. To see those kids so excited . . . those tiny little dudes. Was I ever that small? I don't think so. Kids always make me feel special. They love you the way you are."

Kevin has retained a child's enthusiasm for things important to him that adults often lose. He enjoys tinkering with hand-operated, remote-controlled racers he's built, and he has constructed an aluminum boat, about 2½ feet by 3 feet, elaborately designed and fuel efficient. Kevin also loves to listen to music — "jazz, rap, whatever's good." He has a boat, a Duckworth, of course, which he relishes taking out on the Columbia. The dogs, a Doberman and two Rottweilers, are a passion. "They're great pets," Kevin says. "I love them. I like to train them. They listen to me like nobody does. They get excited to see you. They're your friends no matter what."

As a kid, Kevin loved working with his hands, building and fixing things, and he still does. He worked at Burger King while in high school, but his real job was building furniture. He made money and built self-esteem by paneling his parents' home and building coffee tables, end tables, and chairs. It's a matter of personal pride with Kevin that he can get the job done himself. He has trouble understanding people who don't know a crescent wrench from a pair of needle-nose pliers.

Basketball, working with his hands, boating, music, dogs — Kevin likes many things — everything except the adult fans and members of the media who harp about his weight and criticize his play. He has heard a lot of that since arriving in Portland in a trade with San Antonio during the 1986-87 season. Good enough to play in the NBA All-Star Game twice, including the 1990-91 season, he has often caught the wrath of Blazer fans who see him as too heavy, too moody, too inconsistent.

"People think this is a cakewalk," Kevin says. "It's not easy. It's so stressful, sometimes I wish I could walk away from it for awhile. It's a job with a lot of pressure, a lot of frustrations, a lot of things people don't appreciate." He has told a writer he wanted a more stress-free job in his next life, "a worm farmer or something," and it's clear he's a sensitive person in a game where a little callousness can come in handy.

Duck sometimes gets himself into trouble with his facial expressions on the court. He will complain about

Beyond question Kevin is one of the game's more sensitive souls. Inconsistent play has, at times, left him depressed. ▲ Kevin Duckworth uses his patented hook shot to score a pair on the Warriors. ▶

calls, pout about not getting the ball enough, and occasionally appear to put his personal feelings above the team's welfare. Then he gets criticized. The criticism may have played a part in his disappointing play during the 1991 play-offs, when he shot only 40 percent from the floor and averaged less than 11 points per game.

"I show my feelings," Kevin says. "That can hurt. It hurts me in Portland. People don't want to see your feelings. All people want to see is smiles. I'm here to do a job, and I'm serious about it. I don't want to look bad, I don't want to play bad, I don't want to be outplayed. If I'm happy, I'm happy. If I'm upset, you'll know it."

Weight has been a particularly sensitive subject. He was 330 pounds at one point in his college career at Eastern Illinois and was still over 300 when he arrived in Portland from San Antonio. He worked hard to get it down to 270 his second year, but there have been times when it has slipped back up to the 300 range. He'd rather not discuss it, but he knows it's like the tail that will always wag behind him.

"The weight has always been a part of my relationship with the fans," he says. "They get on me big-time about that. Everybody has his idea on how much I should weigh, what I should look like, but nobody wants to ask me how I feel about it. It hurt me for so many years. That's why I don't listen to people anymore."

He was always the "biggest kid," he remembers, "bigger than the teachers, too. It bothered me a lot. Girls would make fun of me. They were always talking crazy about me because I was so big. I was never skinny a day in my life—not on the day I was born. All the way since grade school, people told me I was too big to be playing. Sometimes when I hear it now, I go off. They don't have a clue what it takes to be a competitive center in this league. I might not be a great center, but I'm a darn good, competitive center."

Kevin, the son of Edward and Maxine Duckworth, grew up in Dolton, Illinois, a suburb of Chicago. Both parents worked to provide a comfortable middle-class life for their four children. Kevin says he wasn't a kid who got into a lot of trouble. He learned from his older brothers, Eddie and Ray. "I saw them do things, and I learned from them not to make the same mistakes."

It is only in recent years that Kevin and his father have really gotten to know each other. Edward was on the road quite a bit, driving truck. The one thing they did together was fish, one of the reasons Kevin loves to fish today. "As a kid, I was intimidated by him," Duck says. "My father raised his voice. He was gruff, and it seemed like I was always listening to him holler. He never put a hand on me, but he did holler. In high school, I started fishing with him and got opportunities to talk to him one-on-one. We're way closer now."

Kevin has always been close to his mother. "My mom's a great lady," he says. "She's like my best friend. She's down-to-earth." Kevin's mother put up with his shooting baskets outside her bedroom window. Her patience

Duck wins a battle for the ball with Detroit's Joe Dumars. ◄ *Here, he snuggles with actress Jasmine Guy, who sang the national anthem before a Blazer game. Kevin worked on carpentry projects as a kid and still enjoys constructing remote-controlled, gas-powered racers. "You'd be amazed how many people don't know how to do anything working with their hands," he says. "I don't intend to take my car to the gas station to change the oil if I don't have to. I'm not spoiled like that." ▲*

Who is dribbling that ball? Maybe there has always been an Isiah Thomas lurking inside Kevin's 7-foot frame. ▲ Blazer dancer Denise Allen rejoices as things go right for the Red, Black, and White. ▶

helped her son become one of the best-shooting big men in the game today. "It'd be real late, and she'd be in bed, and I'd just shoot all night long. I had this thing about not liking the ball to hit the rim at all. If it wasn't all net, I didn't like it."

Despite his size, Kevin is well coordinated. "I was never goofy or clumsy," he says. But instant success did not come. As a 6-4 ninth-grader, the biggest kid in school, he was cut. "It tore my heart out. I was totally crushed. I told my mom I didn't want to play again."

But the next year, a new coach, Bob Sullivan, came to Thornridge High. He talked to the three Duckworth boys—Eddie and Ray weren't playing, either—and persuaded them to go out for the team. Kevin played junior varsity as a sophomore, emerged as a junior, and had an excellent senior season. By that time, Georgetown and Villanova were expressing interest, but Kevin had already committed to Eastern Illinois.

"My favorite teacher [at Thornridge High] was Miss Williams—she got married and her name is Mrs. Reed now," Kevin recalls. "Eastern Illinois kept sending me letters, and the coach came down to see me a lot, and one day I told her about it. She said, 'I went there. It's a great school. You should visit.' I did and I fell in love with it."

Duckworth's memories of his years at Eastern are good. The Panthers lost their first 12 games his freshman year, but four years later they were a winner. As a senior, Duck averaged 19.5 points and 9.1 rebounds and shot a sizzling .631 from the field. In one coaches' association poll, he was voted the most underrated player in the country, and after playing well in post-season camps, he was taken in the second round of the draft, number 33 overall, by San Antonio. Ironically, Kevin had expected to go to Portland with the 24th selection. "I was disappointed Portland didn't take me like they said they would," Duck says. "They picked that tall overseas guy, and my mouth dropped." The tall overseas guy was Arvydas Sabonis, the 7-4 Soviet who has yet to play a minute in the NBA and, by all indications, never will.

Duckworth played only 14 games with the Spurs before coming to Portland in a deal that sent the Blazers' first-round choice, Walter Berry, to San Antonio. It proved to be one of the best trades in Portland's franchise history. However, a sense of insecurity still haunts Kevin's basketball career. After the 1989-90 season, he was convinced he was going to be traded, probably in a deal bringing Houston's Hakeem Olajuwon to Portland. Then, after his discouraging performance in the 1990-91 play-offs, Duck again feared a trade, until the Blazers management assured him that his fears were groundless.

This was good news for Kevin, who realizes he is, at times, his own worst enemy. He desperately wants to win the approval of the fans. He wants to win a championship with the Blazers. He likes living in Oregon. The purchase of the house in Beaverton is proof. "I'll always be from Chicago," he says, "but I have my home here, and it's not temporary. I plan on staying."

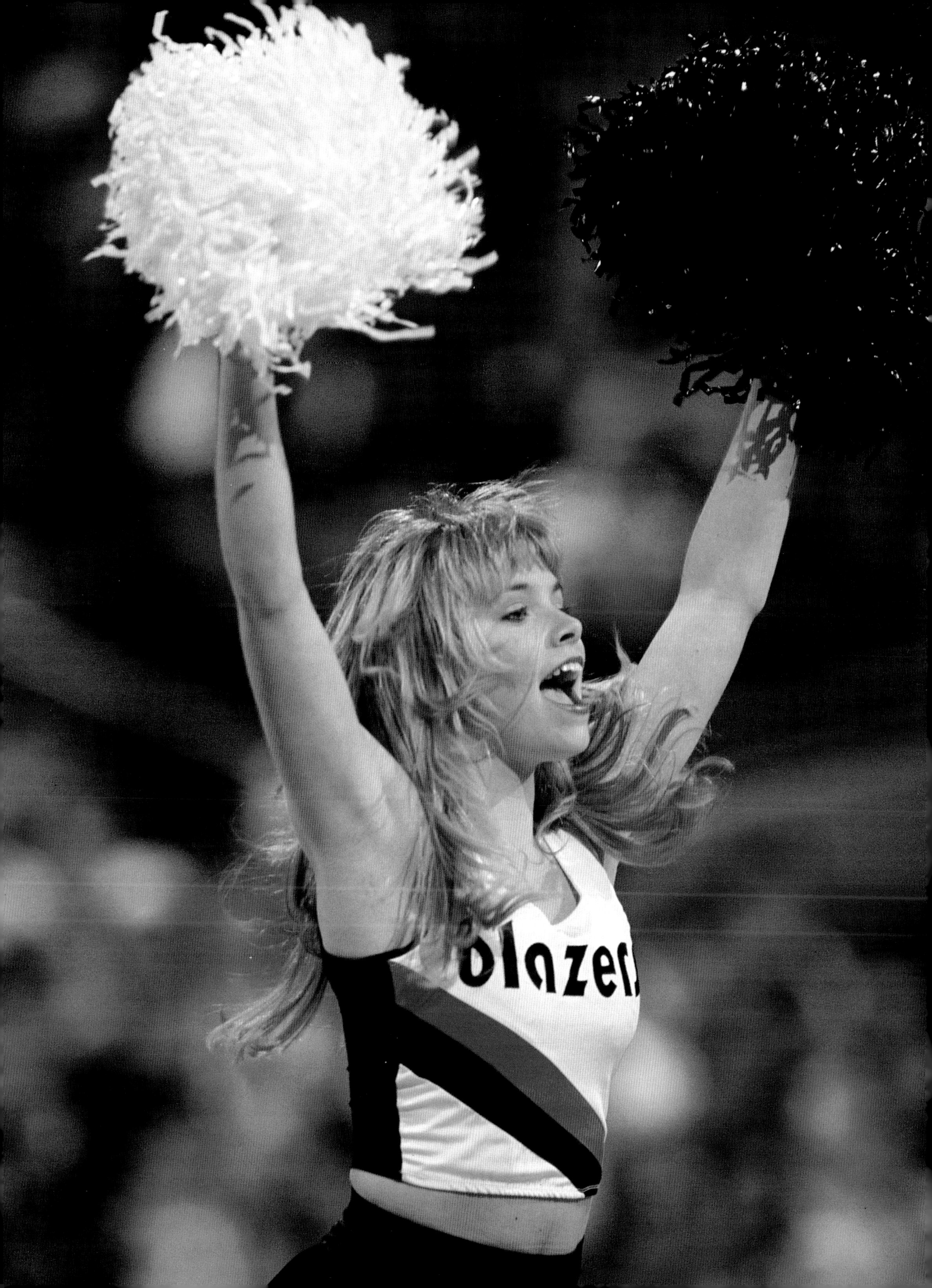
blazers

Cliff Robinson

It's Game 6 of the Western Conference finals series with the Los Angeles Lakers. The Blazers trail 89-88 in the final minute when Terry Porter tips a Magic Johnson pass, chases the ball down, and torpedoes upcourt into what turns out to be a 4-on-1 fast break.

Porter, instead of pushing the ball to Robinson, gives it to Kersey, who fires it to Cliff, who is ready to slam dunk it . . . until it bounces off his hands out of bounds. The Lakers win the game and the series, 4 games to 2, and the Blazers are left to wonder what might have been.

Two months later, like all Blazer players and fans, Cliff Robinson hasn't forgotten The Play. "It was a hard pass. I was really expecting to get the ball first from Terry. When he got it to Jerome, I looked up for a split second at the basket, and that's when Jerome passed it to me. I wish I hadn't looked up."

The 24-year-old Buffalo native, clearly one of the best reserves in the league, raised his numbers from his rookie season in nearly every statistical category, providing the Blazers with consistent inside production off the bench. The 6-10 front-line player accents his versatility by playing all three inside positions, and continues his progress as one of the league's best young front-court defenders. And there's a feeling the best is yet to come. "I think I can be a great player in this league," Cliff says. "I want to be a more tenacious rebounder. I want to be a better free-throw shooter. I want to help us win a championship."

Perhaps the most important thing Robinson did during his second season in Portland was to maintain a low-key profile off the court. That was critical after a rookie season marred by an incident during Portland's first-round play-off series with Dallas, when an argument at a nightclub led to a minor assault charge. After a regular season in which, as a second-round draft choice, he stepped into Coach Rick Adelman's regular rotation and played more than any Blazer rookie in six years, the incident knocked the wind out of Robinson's sails. "That was the lowest part of the year for me," Cliff recalls. "It jolted me. I learned I have to make better decisions."

If there's one characteristic that distinguishes Cliff from the rest of the Blazers, it's his on-court scowl. Sonny Liston should have looked so mean. It comes out when's he mad at Adelman or mad at the referees, mad at the way he's playing or mad that his headband isn't fitting quite right, or mad maybe at the way the moon is in alignment some particular night.

"It's something for on the court," says Cliff with a disarming smile. "When we'd play ball as kids, the older guys used to try to punk me off and make me look like a chump. I had to develop something on the court to make them think I was tough." Some of the impassioned, almost violent, fire Cliff possesses for his game was born out of the hours he spent battling the older kids playing basketball.

Life has not always been smooth for him. His parents, Helena and Clifford Robinson, Sr., separated when he was young, and his father died when Cliff was 10. Helena

Cliff Robinson uses his first-rate mobility to take the ball to the well for two points. ◄ Cliff is one of the league's bright young talents, a player who is versatile, plays excellent defense, and is capable of scoring—as he does here against the Seattle Super Sonics. ▲

51

worked at Bethlehem Steel, then served as a personal-care assistant at a nursing home and raised four of her five children by herself until remarrying years later. There were a lot of mouths to feed and a lot of kids to care for on a stringent budget.

Mother and son are very close, and Cliff is protective of her, particularly since she underwent a mastectomy three years ago. His cousin, Yvonne, who grew up with him, died of cancer at age 28. This has made Cliff painfully aware of a dreaded disease. Recently, he began to help the American Cancer Society raise funds.

Almost 6 feet tall in eighth grade and taunted by kids because of his height, Cliff's early love was football. "They used to call me everything," he recalls. "'Clifford the Big Red Dog, dork . . .' They liked to make fun of me. I think sports helped me through it."

He was junior-varsity quarterback as a sophomore at Riverside High School and dreamed of leading the Buffalo Bills to a Super Bowl crown. But by the time he was a junior and 6-8, Cliff had grown out of football and had turned to basketball, another of his loves. He became a terror on the courts, averaging nearly 30 points a game and drawing nationwide recruiting attention. According to Coach Tony Panzica, Cliff could jump, shoot and—for a big kid—really handle the ball.

Spurring Billy Tubbs at Oklahoma, he attended the University of Connecticut because "I wanted Ma to be able to see me play." But he goofed off and tried to transfer after he became academically ineligible to play. It was only after his mother told him, "No, you can't come back here," that he straightened out and went on to lead the Huskies to the National Invitation Tournament title.

He was one of the seniors the NBA brought to New York on draft day, and he fully expected to be a first-round choice. After the round was completed and he was one of a handful of players still unchosen, he returned to his hotel room, a teapot ready to explode. "I was hot," he says. "I was stunned." Then Rick Adelman was on the phone, welcoming him to the Blazers.

During his first two years in Portland, Robinson went from an unknown to a cherished commodity, a cornerstone of the Blazers' future. He has had his differences with Adelman at times, but he knows his contributions are appreciated by the Blazer coach, who loves his versatility and defensive prowess. If there's a problem with his rapid progression from rookie to year two, it's the thought he won't be satisfied until he's a starter.

Cliff definitely wants to be a starter sometime in his career, but he says firmly, "If we're winning, and everybody is playing well, you don't want to rock the boat. I want to play, but I want us to be a winning team."

Robinson has become a favorite of the fans, who marvel at his athletic moves and spectacular dunks. In turn, he loves the fans. "It's great to know you're appreciated. It makes you want to go out on the floor and show them you're worthy." If he has put his off-court problems behind him, that's a good first step.

Will it be red, black, or white? That was the question of the Blazer fans who sat behind the team's bench and emulated the flavor of the headband their hero wore when he entered the game. "I just like the feel of it," explains Cliff, who doesn't need the headband to keep the hair out of his eyes. ▲ His fans were equally creative. ▶

Danny Ainge

The tip-off for Game 6 of the 1991 Western Conference finals in the L.A. Forum is only moments away. The Lakers lead the Blazers three games to two in the best-of-seven series. If the Blazers steal this one, they return to Portland for a deciding game that will be very difficult for the Lakers to win. The pressure is so thick, you couldn't chip it with a chisel. "Guys' stomachs are in knots," says Drexler. "They're all taking antacid tablets. If you're not just a little bit nervous, you're not ready to play."

Danny Ainge is ready—he's played in hundreds of big games during his basketball career—but he doesn't look nervous. He sidles over to actor/Laker fanatic Jack Nicholson, who is in his customary seat by the visitors' bench. Danny tells him, "It's been fun, Jack, but your season is over. We're going to win tonight and then we're going to win Game 7."

Nicholson gets the last laugh. The Lakers build an early lead, then hang onto it to win 91-90 and wrap up the series. For Ainge, a third championship ring will have to wait another year, and he is dejected.

Soon, however, the boy is back in Danny. It's his first Oregon summer in a while, and he takes advantage of it, biking and swimming; playing tennis, softball, and golf; and enjoying life with his wife, Michelle, and their four children. A legend at North Eugene High School in the late 1970s and arguably the greatest high school athlete in Oregon's history, Danny Ainge has come home. The Sacramento Kings traded him to the Blazers before the 1990-91 season. Ainge did his part to help a great team win 63 regular-season games and advance to within a smidgen of a second successive conference crown.

Seems like yesterday that the mop-topped Ainge was weaving his magic for North Eugene. He was an outstanding baseball player and football quarterback and receiver—the very best of the greatest senior class in the state's history, all-state in three sports both his junior and senior years—but basketball was his game.

Danny was the third of four children born to Don and Kay Ainge, a butcher-turned-insurance man and a housewife. The bills were always paid, food was always on the table, but money was tight. "I remember we had a family meeting," Danny recalls. "Dad said we had $30 to spend on entertainment for the entire summer. We voted to use it to buy a family swim pass at the YMCA."

Athletic pursuits were the family's byword. "I don't remember wanting to do anything but play ball as a kid," Danny says. He and his older brothers, Doug and David, were jocks from the get-go. It was one of the reasons Danny became an outstanding athlete—he was always trying to keep up with his older brothers.

Heavily recruited by major colleges in three sports, Danny signed a baseball contract with the Toronto Blue Jays and played college basketball at Brigham Young University. It was there he met his wife, Michelle Toolson, a pert, bubbly bookend to his boundless enthusiasm.

College basketball was a rousing success for Ainge, who was named Eastman National Player of the Year his

A welcome addition to the Blazers, on and off the court, was Danny Ainge. ◄ Ainge bounced into his role as the team's third guard with a flourish, spelling both Drexler and Porter, providing leadership and scoring punch. A Eugene native, he was thrilled to be playing with the team he had rooted for as a kid. ▲

senior season. Who can forget the incredible coast-to-coast drive for a basket that beat Notre Dame in the NCAA tournament, a film clip that will be shown on highlight tapes forever? Pro baseball was another story. He missed spring training every year because of basketball and never reached his potential.

When Danny signed with Toronto, he agreed not to play pro basketball, but the Boston Celtics, gambling they could spring him from his contract, chose him in the second round of the 1981 draft. The gamble paid off. Danny played 7½ seasons, helping his team win two NBA titles and reach the finals four straight seasons.

About the time he signed with the Celtics, Danny endured his biggest personal tragedy. In 1982, his mother, Kay, committed suicide. "It was very traumatic," recalls Danny. "It made me sit back and think about what life is really all about. It made me want to try to be the person I want to be so I will never to go through the depression my mom went through." His father says, "Danny was very strong. He was very supportive of me."

Throughout his career, Ainge proved himself a great competitor, an outstanding perimeter shooter, and a leader. He also gained a reputation as a bad boy.

During Danny's second season, 7-1, the 240-pound Rollins gave Danny elbows as he moved around the Hawk center's picks. Finally, Ainge tackled him. Players from both teams joined in, and Rollins bit Ainge's right hand. Danny needed five stitches and was ejected from the game, but after reviewing tapes, the league office ruled that Rollins had precipitated the incident. Unfortunately, Ainge is remembered as the one who did the biting.

Ainge has committed hard fouls now and then to prevent a player from converting a basket. K. C. Jones, formerly Ainge's coach at Boston, defends him. "He is not a dirty player. You have to understand what a totally determined kind of ballplayer Danny Ainge is."

"Look, I'm intense, but I play within the rules," says Danny. "The way I learned it in my backyard, if you're playing one-on-one and the guy's going in for an easy shot to win the game, you foul him. I take smart fouls. I would never try to hurt anybody."

Throughout his first season in Portland, Ainge was a model of decorum. He didn't get a technical foul all season. The scowl rarely emerged. Danny admits he intentionally cleaned up his act a bit. "I guess I just tried to be the other way and balance things a little. And I think I needed to be an example to some of the young guys."

If there's one thing Danny has, it's balance in his life. A hard-nosed competitor, he has an impish sense of humor. His Mormon faith is important to him. He is a stake missionary who meets monthly with six families in his church, and he gives 10 percent of his salary. Family is his focal point. The four Ainge children—Ashlee, 12; Austin, 10; Tanner, 7; and Taylor, 4—keep Danny and Michelle on their toes inside and outside their Portland home. Danny hopes to play with the Blazers to the end of the trail. He is proof you *can* come home again.

*A*inge ranks second on the all-time NBA list for the most three-point field goals in a career and was a major weapon for the Blazers, finishing sixth in the league's individual statistics in shooting threes. ▲ He never professed to own the quicks of a Michael Jordan, but Ainge is a smart defender who rarely gets burned. ▶

Mark Bryant

Need an escort through a dark alley in a rough part of town? Mark Bryant would be just about anybody's pick. At 6-9 and 250, his square-jawed face decorated by a Van Dyke goatee, Bryant looks menacing. "Very intimidating," says his wife, Shelley, an amused grin on her face. Mark is not oblivious to his appearance. "If you looked at me, you'd say, 'He's evil,'" Bryant says. "Everybody thinks that until they get to know me."

That, in itself, is not easy. Polite and easy-going, Bryant is one of the most reserved of the Trail Blazers. It's difficult to pierce his veneer and get to know the real man. And another thing: you don't get to make the decision about getting to know Mark Bryant. He does.

"He sits back and observes," says Shelley, who met Mark his junior year at Seton Hall, then married him in 1989. "Sometimes it's for a few minutes or an hour, sometimes it's for a year or two. That way he can pick up on your personality and attitude and tell if he wants to be friends." If Bryant chooses to reveal himself, you find a warm, fun-loving player with inner strength and integrity.

Mark needed every ounce to get through 1989-90, his second season in Portland. It began when his Portland apartment burned shortly after he was married. It continued with the near-fatal accident of teammate and close friend, Ramon Ramos. It reached its nadir when his mother, Harriet, and Ora, his god-mother aunt, were killed in a car accident in his native New Jersey.

The emotional scars from the death of his mother and aunt remain with Bryant today. "I still haven't gotten through that," he says. "It hurts me to sit down and think about it. I still can't believe they're gone."

His mother was a certified nurse, and Mark describes her as outgoing. "She'd do anything for anybody. She was always very protective. She didn't really want me to have girlfriends, and it was rough for me and Shelley at one point. But that was my mom. I miss her a lot."

His father, Levi Bryant, is a maintenance man in a South Orange high school. "My father's real quiet," says Mark. "He sits back and observes. You can't tell what he's thinking, but he's a strong person. We've become closer since my mother passed away."

The lives of the Bryant children—Mark is the third of four kids—revolved around playground sports and activities. Always bigger than the others, Mark took to football first, but gave it up in high school to concentrate on basketball. By the time he was a senior, he was a 6-8 post man, heavily recruited by all the major powers of the East. He considered South Carolina, Louisville, Ohio State, and Maryland. Seton Hall's program was down, and he said, "No way in the world am I going there."

But Coach P. J. Carlesimo was persistent. In the end, Bryant chose Seton Hall because his parents could see him play, and he could get lots of court time and Big East attention. A perimeter player who liked to float outside to shoot jumpers, Bryant started all four years. Carlesimo began bringing in more talent—players such as John Morton and Ramos—and the Pirates started winning.

Mark Bryant has two main goals this season. He intends to "take some heads off" with his physical play, and he wants to help the Blazers win a title. ◄ A series of bad breaks have helped derail Bryant's plans thus far. ▲ The best-laid strategies don't always work, but the Blazers try to be prepared for anything. Rick Adelman is one of the best coaches in basketball for drawing up final-second plays in crucial situations. ► ►

59

In his senior year, Mark was an All-Big East selection, leading Seton Hall to the school's first-ever NCAA berth.

Bryant, a first-round pick in 1988, started as the Blazers' power forward the first half of his rookie season under Coach Mike Schuler, but his initial year was less than a smashing success. He averaged only 5.0 points and 3.2 rebounds, and was injured late in the season, breaking a thumb in a fight with Boston's Joe Kleine. "I wasn't ready mentally to be a starter," he says. "There I was, handling money, with my own apartment, a car and a whole bunch of things to do, all for the first time. It was a tough situation for me."

The next season, Bryant came to training camp 20 pounds lighter. "Everybody told me how big I was," he says, "but I didn't feel it, you know? That is, until I dropped the weight. Then I said, 'Oh yeah.'" It didn't show immediately. He played fewer minutes his second season, averaging only 2.9 points and 2.5 rebounds, and he missed games due to his mother's death and the accident involving Ramon. Mark suffered along with Ramon's family but was a comforting influence.

Through it all, Shelley tried to let Mark be himself. "I knew he'd handle it," she says. "He's a strong man." Even so, Mark found himself breaking into tears, and his feelings carried over to inadequate play on the court. "Once you lose your confidence, it's real hard to play," Bryant explains. "It seems like everybody's watching you. You make a mistake and you worry about what people are thinking. You have to get that out of your mind."

He played well in training camp before the 1990-91 season and worked his way into Coach Rick Adelman's regular rotation. He was playing the best ball of his pro career—averaging 5 points and 3.7 rebounds, and shooting .478 from the field and .723 from the foul line—when he broke the fifth metatarsal in his right foot in a February game against the Lakers. "Sometimes I wonder if I'm jinxed," he said at the time. He missed 27 games, and, though he returned in April, he never really regained his form and had no major role in the play-offs.

Bryant rarely shows emotion on the court and almost never draws a technical foul call. Off the court, with friends, he's more revealing. "I like to kid and fool around," he admits. Mark gives Shelley points for good influence. "She reminds me of my mother. She never takes any crap, but I'm always testing."

The Bryants make their home in South Orange, New Jersey, just a twenty-minute drive to New York City. In Portland, Mark likes to tool around in his '90 Jeep Cherokee, his '84 Porsche 928, or his '89 BMW 750. He and Shelley intend to have children eventually, but neither one of them is quite ready yet to give up their freedom.

Bryant intends "to really take some heads off this year. Before I finish, I will be one of the bigger-name power forwards in the league, one of the elite guys at my position." That amounts to as much of a speech as Mark Bryant usually gives. His coaches, of course, would like nothing better than to see him fulfill his prophecy.

Bryant is all business on the court, but despite a quiet demeanor, he enjoys repartee off it. "I open up a lot around my friends," he says. "I like to kid and fool around. I like to be around people—up people." ▲ Bill Schonely is an institution for the Blazers, having served as radio announcer since the club's inception in 1970. ▶

Walter Davis

Walter Davis takes a chair near the floor in Memorial Coliseum and gazes up at the empty seats. "It's a lot different in here now, isn't it?" he says, and indeed it is. The roar of 12,884 spectators turns the Coliseum into a pantheon of the city's basketball gods. Now the stillness is broken only by the voice of the "Greyhound," a man who has been an All-Star six times, who has one of the prettiest jump shots in NBA history, and who has the kind of stroke displayed in coaching videos.

When he went to Denver in 1988 after eleven seasons with the Phoenix Suns, Davis expected to end his career with the Nuggets. Walter and his wife, Susan, whom he married in 1981, liked Denver. They felt it would be a good place to raise their two daughters, Hillary and Jordan. And Denver gave Davis a shot when no other team would. What Davis didn't foresee was his leap from the league's worst team to the best in one stunning swoop.

He was playing well as the 1990-91 campaign began, scoring big numbers in new coach Paul Westhead's speed-game system. In one memorable game against Seattle, he scored 31 second-half points. But the Nuggets were losing, and losing big. Their opponents were trying to be the first to score 200 in a regular-season game.

In January, two weeks before the All-Star break, the Trail Blazers landed Davis in a three-team deal. The Blazers envisioned the 6-6 Davis, who was averaging 18.7 points for Denver at the time, as an insurance policy at off guard and small forward as well as a perimeter-shooting threat off the bench. The problem was that the Blazers didn't have extra minutes floating around for any player, not even a man who ranked nineteenth on the NBA's all-time scoring list with 19,064 points.

Davis has yet to give the Blazers the boost they wanted. He showed flashes, but he struggled with his irregular playing time and missed jumpers he could make with his eyes closed. It was a situation unbefitting to one of the greats of the game, but Davis was at peace with himself. He's glad to be playing pro ball at an age when most players have hung up their sneakers, and he's glad to have the torment of his final years in Phoenix behind him.

Perhaps his grandest achievement was overcoming the drug problem that nearly ended his career in Phoenix. Walter says he began using cocaine in 1978, his second year in the NBA. While it didn't seem to affect his performance on court, it certainly affected his life off court. Twice he turned himself into rehabilitation clinics for cocaine abuse, and after the 1986-87 season, he testified before a grand jury in a narcotics case involving several teammates. Five players were indicted on drug-related charges, including Davis who was named on eight counts but was granted immunity from prosecution.

The Davis image was tainted in the league, and he has worked since that time to restore it. He says he stopped using drugs in 1986. He still attends meetings for those battling addiction and speaks to groups involved in the Adult Substance Abuse Program. "As you get more sobriety," he says, "you don't attend meetings

*W*alter *Davis ranks 20th on the all-time NBA scoring list with more than 19,000 career points, and after 14 seasons in the league, it appears the Greyhound is making his final stop in Portland. After he retires, his laurels will surely land him a spot in the Basketball Hall of Fame, to join Lenny Wilkens as the only men ever to have played with the Blazers and to have been enshrined in the Hall. ◄ Davis watches action from the bench with friend Wayne Cooper, a teammate in Denver.* ▲

65

as much, but I think it's important to go to remind yourself of where you've been."

Davis grew up in the rural South. His father, Edward, worked with a trucking company. His mother, Gertrude, did domestic work. Walter was the youngest of thirteen children, and, he laughs, the spoiled baby. They were all crowded into a small, Pineville, North Carolina, home. Hand-me-downs and simple meals were the bill of fare at the Davises, but Walter recalls what he considers a wonderful childhood.

Edward and Gertrude Davis were very special people, "Christians who taught all of us to be unselfish and show consideration for other people. They never said anything negative about anyone."

Walter has always been among the most fit of NBA players, even at his age, and he credits his good genes. "Both my parents had amazing bodies," he says. "They were in their seventies when they died in 1987, but they looked like they were in their fifties."

The one thing Walter craved as a child was the open affection of his father. Though Walter is often on the road in his job, he does what he can to ensure his own children don't miss that in him. "I want to be close to my kids. I always said, when I have kids I'm going to hug them and tell them I love them, because I really missed that."

All the Davis boys played sports, but the baby was the best. Only 5-8 when he started ninth grade, he sprouted like a tobacco plant in the Carolina sun and was 6-4 when he entered his sophomore year at South Mecklenburg High. He says he liked basketball "because you could do it by yourself. All you needed was a goal and a ball. I'd get up early in the morning and shoot for at least two or three hours. Then I'd come back in the afternoon and play until it was dark."

The summer before his freshman year, Davis attended a basketball camp, which changed his life. Former NBA great Dolph Schayes was the shooting instructor and helped Walter develop the famous jump shot. "He thought jump shooting would decrease the chances of someone blocking your shot," explains Walter.

Davis returned to lead South Mecklenburg to two more state crowns. He then signed with the University of North Carolina Tar Heels because he had always wanted to play for Dean Smith. He had an outstanding career, and took Carolina to the NCAA title game as a senior.

After his junior year, Davis made the Olympic team that defeated Yugoslavia for the gold medal. He was picked as the number 5 selection in the 1977 draft by Phoenix, where he became a perennial All-Star for the Suns. But Davis doesn't really like the limelight. He says, "I like a slow pace. I go about my job very quietly."

The 1991-92 season may well be the final one for the Greyhound. He hopes the good things he has accomplished will offset the mistakes. "It's not how you start," he is convinced, "but how you finish your life that counts. You have the beginning, the middle, and the end, and most people will judge you on the end."

When Davis was a young player in the NBA, he "just tried to outrun everybody," with excellent results. Later, he adopted a different style. "I think I set the defender up better now," he says. "I look more for what he's giving me. If he's off me, I'm going to take my jump shot. When I was younger, it didn't matter. I was going to blow around him regardless." ▲ *Baptism under fire: Williams anoints San Antonio's Rod Strickland.* ▶

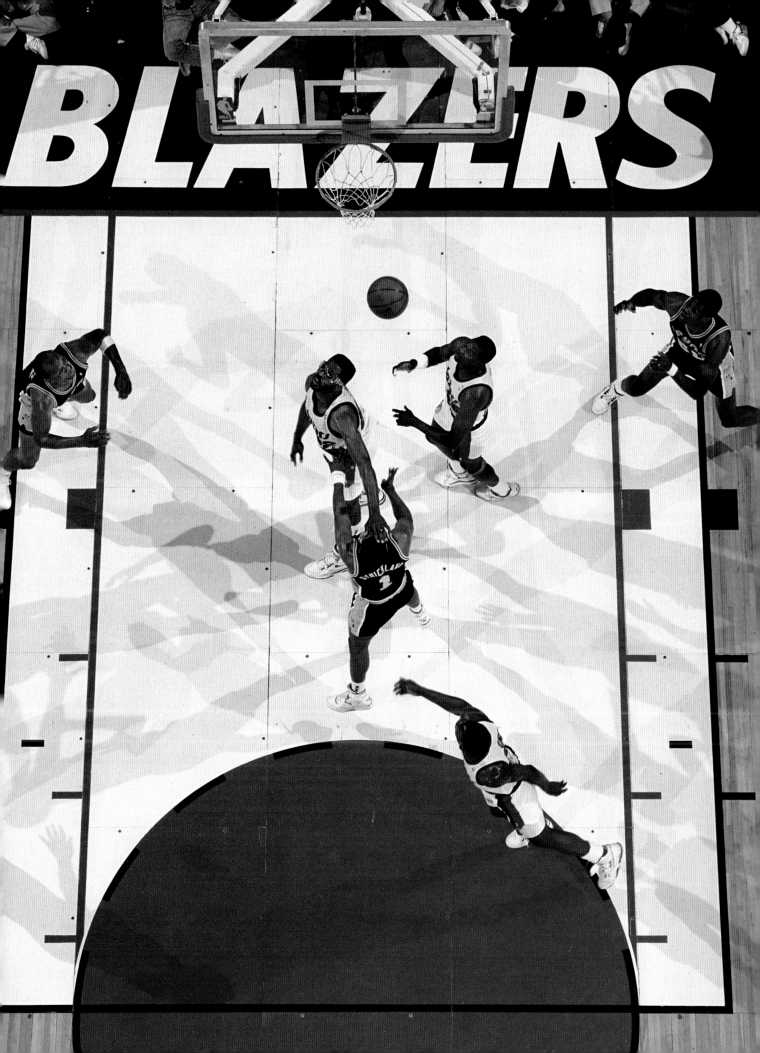

Danny Young

Danny Young sits on the patio of Friday's, a notable eatery and watering hole not far from the home he rents from former Blazer Michael Holton in Tigard, and munches on buffalo wings. He's wearing his Vuarnet shades to protect his eyes, not his identity. The hostess has recognized him, and a few customers cast occasional glances, but that is the extent of the attention he receives. No "Hey, there, Danny!" No autograph requests.

"I can go a lot of places a lot of the guys can't go," he says. "I can walk through a mall, and maybe two or three people will recognize me, whereas a Kevin Duckworth or Clyde Drexler can't go without being mobbed. Michael Jordan, he has to wait until a movie starts and then go sit in the back. Can you imagine that?"

The down-to-earth, soft-spoken Danny Young has been the most anonymous of the Trail Blazers. Normally sized—if you can call 6-4, 175 normal—reserved of personality, and short on extended playing time, Young has bypassed the deluge of fame that has inundated most of the Blazers.

He relishes his privacy, because he is a very private man. In the eyes of the people who make decisions for the Trail Blazers, Danny Young is a good soldier, which is what they want in a back-up point guard who sees mostly spot minutes and, sometimes, no minutes at all.

If Danny is a good soldier, credit his father, Theodore, a 22-year veteran of the armed forces who ended his military career as a master sergeant and spent the last fifteen years of his life as a mailman. Danny and his four siblings grew up in a disciplined atmosphere. Dad dictated that. "He was always big on doing what you're supposed to do, taking responsibility for your actions," Danny says about his father, who died in 1987. "Dad wouldn't let us get into any trouble. We knew if we did, we'd have to answer to him."

His mother, Alice, is a nursing assistant in Raleigh, North Carolina, where Danny and his wife, Deborah, built their dream home in 1991. Danny likes being close to his mom. "Mother is shy," he says. "She worries a lot—I guess all mothers do. She's a good person with a good heart. Both dad and mom supported me in little-league baseball and in basketball. All through high school and college, they came to see my games."

Like many military families, the Youngs were on the move a lot. Danny lived in Michigan and New York before the family settled in Raleigh. His older brothers got him into basketball. "Like all younger brothers," Danny says, "I wanted to follow them around. Then I got to the point where I really liked the game. I guess I was a loner. I used to go out by myself and shoot. It's not like baseball, where you need eight other guys for a team. You can fantasize. You ever see the commercial about the guy playing by himself who gets fouled and makes the last shot to win the game? That was me."

Danny was a fan of David Thompson, but he didn't exactly emulate his hero's style. Young's game has always been more understated and tuned to a lower frequency. If

Danny Young has filled a role for the Blazers the past three seasons, providing them with quality depth and reliable reserve play at point guard. Even so, he almost always comes into fall training camp with a challenge for his position. "It's always going to be like that," Young says. "I've accepted it. I may be underappreciated by outside people, but I think my teammates and coaches appreciate me." ◄ *A backside view of Blazers at attention during the playing of the national anthem.* ▲

there is a similarity, it's Young's flair for last-second shots. He has an uncanny knack for sinking long-range prayers at the ends of quarters. He is probably best known for the shot that didn't count—the game-tying 40-footer at the end of Game 3 of the 1990 NBA Finals, which was eventually ruled *after the buzzer* by referee Earl Strom.

Young may have lacked flash at Enloe High School, but he was an outstanding player. He twice earned all-state honors as a guard-forward type, and averaged 22 points a game as a senior. He played his college ball at Wake Forest, helping the Deacons to 85 wins during a brilliant career.

Danny was chosen in the second round of the draft by Seattle and made the Sonics' roster, but that only set him up for a big fall. The day after he brought Deborah out for a visit, he was released to make room for John Schweitz off the injured reserve list. "It was the first time I'd been told I wasn't good enough to play," he says. "I felt terrible. I kept thinking, 'What am I going to tell Deborah?' Deborah gave me a lot of support."

Young wound up playing for the Wyoming Wildcatters in the CBA. He liked his coach, Jack Schalow, who now is an assistant with the Blazers. Other than that, he says, the best thing about the CBA was he didn't have to play there long. He returned to Seattle for three seasons with the Sonics, then was picked up by the Blazers two days before the 1988-89 season began.

He played well before breaking his wrist and missing half the season, but impressed the brass enough to sign a guaranteed three-year contract. The next year, he backed up Terry Porter at the point, but when the Blazers acquired veteran Danny Ainge, he saw his time drop from an average of 17 minutes a game to less than 12 in 1990-91. "I knew it would cut down on my time," Young says, "but that's the nature of the business. I don't make personnel decisions. If Danny could help us win a championship, more power to him."

Blazer coaches appreciate Young for more than his easy-going nature. He is a smart player who rarely takes a bad shot. He is solid from three-point range, though he shot poorly from the outside in the 1990-91 season. He gets his share of steals, and Coach Adelman considers Danny his best position defender at guard. Young may not light up the scoreboard, but that's not his job.

Danny and Deborah hope to have children someday. "My mother, her parents, everybody back home has been saying, 'When are the kids coming?' Since we built the house, they figure we have to put some kids in it." Sometime, Danny might want to get into coaching, but only at the high school level. "I wouldn't want to coach college," he says. "I wouldn't want to go into somebody's living room and promise the world. The NBA? The egos are too big. But who's to say, if I was one of the stars, I wouldn't have the same problem?"

With Danny Young, the guess is he'd keep the same hat size. He's never been spoiled, he's never been pampered. He's a good soldier, and that's the way he likes to be.

*B*azer fans had a letter for Karl "The Mailman" Malone to deliver during the 1991 play-offs. ▲ Danny tries to deliver whatever Coach Adelman asks of him, but it's rarely scoring a basket. "I know my role," Young says. "I try to keep everybody involved, which is tough, because you have a lot of egos out there. I think I've showed I want to do whatever it takes to win." ▶

Wayne Cooper

Denise Cooper is out on this early summer afternoon, and Wayne Cooper is playing Mr. Mom in their spacious Portland home. His two youngest daughters are home with the chicken pox. Good thing Pop already had it.

Wayne loves being a father to his three girls, Courtney, 10; Andrea, 6; and Lauren, 3. For more than eight months of the year, while he's playing with the Trail Blazers, Wayne is in and out of their lives. The summers are family time. The Coopers travel and play and have fun together. "I try to spend a lot of time with my kids," Cooper says. He also loves to spend time with his wife, whom he met at the University of New Orleans and whom he calls the "perfect companion."

Wayne is an anomaly in the world of professional sports—unassuming, almost devoid of ego. He is as nice to the locker room attendant as he is to his teammates. "There are enough jerks out there," he says. "You don't have to be a jerk in life."

Cooper is arguably the most private of the Blazers. He is shy. He struggles to endure the never-ending, all-consuming interest of Blazer fans. He is looking forward to being out of the public eye.

That may be soon. At 35, the 6-10 Cooper is in his fourteenth NBA season, his fifth in two stints in Portland. He's lost a step, and he never was that quick to begin with. The 1991-92 season will probably be his last, but he can look back on a long, esteemed career with pride.

Credit his determination. "I've always been an underdog," he says. "There's always been somebody saying I can't do what I want to do. That's the biggest force driving me."

Wayne was the fifth of six children born to Artis and Mamie Cooper. Artis was a factory worker. Mamie was a housewife. "She was a great lady," Cooper says. "She was probably my closest friend. She was well-educated, and everybody loved her. One thing I learned from her was a love of little kids. She'd see kids who were hungry and needed help, she'd take them and feed them." Mamie died of kidney and heart trouble in 1988, and it was, Wayne says, "one of the most devastating times of my life." But he believes he grew from it, and it strengthened him overall.

Wayne describes his father as well disciplined. "We all respected him. He made all of us kids work hard."

It was a no-frills household. "We always had our own house," Wayne says. "We always had food. We didn't have extras, but we had a very happy childhood, a very close family."

As a kid, Wayne played a lot of basketball. "I played alone a lot. I wouldn't call myself a loner, but I enjoyed spending time by myself. I remember dreaming a lot. I think kids don't do enough of that today. Always dream and always expect to succeed."

Dreams were often different for black kids. Racism was a fact of life in the South of the 1960s. Wayne and his younger brother, Alvin, integrated an elementary

*S*ometimes getting ready for a game is a stretch for Cooper, who is in his 14th season. His playing time waned last year but not his enthusiasm. "I see a lot of guys who don't play and all they do is complain," he says. "Then they get the opportunity to play and they're out of shape. I'm not going to let that happen." ◄ When he retires, Cooper will miss the game but not the fanfare. "I don't need that part of it," he insists. "I'm going to miss my teammates, the locker room, the competition." ▲

school in McRae at his mother's insistence. At the time, they were being bussed to a school ten miles away, while the school white children attended was within walking distance. "We integrated the school way before its time," Wayne recalls, but it was hard. "Today, I could be a very bitter person, but if I did that, I'd be as ignorant as they were."

As a 6-5 junior at Telfair County High in McRae, Georgia, Wayne made the team but didn't play much. "I couldn't even dunk," he says. "The only thing I could do — and I remember this vividly — is block shots. I had a natural gift for that." The next year, Cooper became adept at rebounding, but he was still an underdog. In one game early in the season, he collected 15 points and 15 rebounds against one of the best teams in the conference, and the coach told him it had been luck. "I don't know if he meant it," Wayne says, "but it pushed me. I remember coming back and having another big game."

By his sophomore season at the University of New Orleans, Cooper had earned the team's most valuable player award. Coach Butch Van Breda Kolff alerted NBA scouts he had something special, and Wayne was taken in the second round by Golden State. "I was a long shot," he says, "but something deep inside got me through." He made the NBA's All-Rookie team and went on to play for six NBA teams. His career scoring average is only 8 points a game, but he's always been a capable rebounder and an outstanding shot-blocker, swatting more than 1,500 shots during his NBA career.

Cooper played two seasons in Portland, 1982-83 and 1983-84, before moving to Denver in a trade. After the 1988-89 season with the Nuggets, Cooper was a free agent, and he was thrilled when the Blazers signed him to a three-year deal.

Cooper knew he was taking on a lesser role when he came to Portland, but he figured his body couldn't handle a lot of minutes, and he liked the way Rick Adelman was a player's coach. During the 1990-91 season, Wayne played just 746 regular-season minutes, but he handled it beautifully because he is a pro who understands not everybody can play.

That, however, doesn't mean it's easy. "You get to this level because you have somewhat of an ego," Cooper observes. "The thing I want to do is be ready if Rick needs me. I see a lot of guys who don't play, and then they get the opportunity to play and they're out of shape. I'm not going to let that happen."

Cooper has worked hard to prepare for the 1991-92 season. He has also worked hard to prepare himself for life after basketball. "A lot of guys who retired are struggling because they were caught up in being in the limelight. I don't need that part of it. But I'm going to miss my teammates, the locker room, the competition."

Cooper doesn't plan to hold a press conference to announce his retirement. He intends to leave the game the same way he entered it. "I'll wake up and say, 'That's it,'" he says. "I just want to quietly walk away."

There are plenty of happy moments for the Wayne Cooper family, from left Courtney, 10; Denise with Lauren, 3; Wayne and Andrea, 6. ▲ Wayne Cooper battles Minnesota's Felton Spencer for a rebound. ▶

Alaa Abdelnaby

Alaa Abdelnaby loves to talk, and he does it well. Bright, funny, and articulate, he majored in political science and minored in communications at Duke University, and it shows. If he ever becomes a starter in the NBA, he is someone sportswriters will seek out for interviews.

The "if" is what concerns Alaa now. He knew he'd have to be patient and ride the bench a lot during his rookie season with the Trail Blazers in 1990-91, but that doesn't mean he liked it. "I'm discouraged," he says, reflecting on a regular season in which he spent only 290 minutes on the court, almost all in garbage time. "It's hard when you don't play. Next to going into a game when you're ahead by 20 points, the hardest thing is going in when you're down by 20. You lose your self-worth a little bit."

The words sound harsher than does Alaa. The season has been fun, and no one enjoys a laugh more than this 23-year-old. What has been hard are the changes: from the East Coast to the West Coast; from starter to last-line reserve; from son and scholarship athlete to a young man on his own for the first time.

Abdelnaby didn't expect to immediately move ahead of the veterans in Coach Adelman's playing rotation—Kevin Duckworth and Wayne Cooper at center, Buck Williams, Mark Bryant, and Cliff Robinson at power forward—but he thought he'd have some chances. Save for a memorable performance against Karl Malone in a victory over the Jazz at Utah, he didn't.

Each Blazer regular—even Drexler—began his career on the bench. Mostly, Abdelnaby did his best with a support role. That doesn't make it easier to accept. "I'm here in Oregon to do one thing," Alaa says. "I don't have family. I don't have long-time friends. I'm here to play basketball. I'm not mad about anything, but I'm impatient. I want everything yesterday."

Blazer coaches remind him that his rookie season is a learning process, but Alaa has a dream: "to be a starter on the type of team the Blazers are now—a team that wins almost every game."

His father, Abdelhamid Abdelnaby, left his family home in Egypt to experience the American dream. He landed in New Jersey and, after securing employment as a lab technician and then as an engineer, he returned for wife Ferial and Alaa, his 2-year-old son. Eventually, the Abdelnabys had three more children and became successful business people and proud Americans. At the same time, they maintained their Arabic language and their religion: Alaa remains a Muslim.

"I'm close to mom," says Alaa. "She's my shoulder to cry on, my best friend. We're very open with each other. My dad is a proud guy. I've never met anyone with such pride—in himself, in his family. Even so, he'll let me make my mistakes before he'll interfere. When I cried before I left for college my freshman year, he laughed at me. 'You gotta be tough,' he said, and he's every bit of that. He's a rough and tough kind of guy. As much as I love my mom, if I could be half the man my father is, I'd be happy."

Alaa Abdelnaby didn't play much as a rookie last season, but give him time. He says, "I hope someday I'll have a chance to make a name for myself." ◄ Abdelnaby's wit and personality have already made him a favorite with teammates and the media, including NBC's Dick Enberg, with whom he shares a joke. ▲

As a youngster, Alaa was not quite Prince Charming. "I was tall," he says. "I was clumsy. I was insecure. A good friend drew a picture of me, and there was nothing but legs. I was the one the girls never talked to—never."

His senior year, girls at Bloomfield High started to look, and so did college recruiters. Alaa averaged 28 points, 18 rebounds, and 9 blocked shots a game. Bloomfield won the county title, and the coaches began drooling, but it was Duke's Mike Krzyzewski who won the recruiting battle.

"I remember the first time I saw him," Abdelnaby says. "In walks this little guy with a big nose. We sit down and talk, and we clicked. To this day, he's by far the most honest person I've met in my life. If it comes down to telling you something and making you cry, he'll tell you. Not many people are like that. At first, you hate him for it. After a while, you start respecting him."

Coach K's honesty intrigued Alaa. "One time he visited our school, and I didn't have a ride home and asked him for a lift. We lived about two miles down the road. He said, 'I can't do that. NCAA rules.' I looked at him like, are you kidding? You won't drive me two miles? Who's going to know? But something in me liked that."

The young man with the strict upbringing and toe-the-line coach nevertheless struggled through most of his career at Duke, both on and off the court, and didn't become a full-time starter until his senior season.

He got on poorly with the Blue Devils' star, Danny Ferry. "Danny and I had a hard time," Abdelnaby says. "It was nobody's fault. I was his personal screener. We're both playing inside, and he's getting the ball every time. I wasn't resentful as much as insubordinate at times. I felt . . . I wasn't getting enough opportunity to grow into a role. We used to fight, throw punches, but I've never hated Danny Ferry. I don't wish bad things for him."

Duke made it to the NCAA Final Four in each of Alaa's last three seasons. When Ferry departed, Alaa came into his own as a senior. Suddenly, he was the go-to guy, averaging 15.1 points and shooting 62 percent from the floor. "I've always been somebody who loved pressure," he says. "It makes me play better. The big games—they're fun."

Alaa fit in well with the Blazers as their only rookie. He didn't get hazed or asked to sing his alma mater, but there were rituals the veterans imposed. "I got to bring out the balls at the beginning of practice. I had to get Clyde his donuts for a while. That's fine. The guys accepted me. They've been great." Alaa has just about everything he wants: a college degree, finished in summer-school correspondence; a black Porsche 928; a good job; and a loving, supportive family. What he really wants and doesn't yet have is a place among the NBA elite.

"The money's great," Alaa says, "but I don't play basketball so I can hop in my Porsche and go get another one. I love to play the game. I think about being like Buck—power forward on the world's best team. Those are my dreams. I think, someday, I'll get there."

Abdelnaby tests Danny Ainge in a pre-game check for mumps. Alaa watched Ainge for years as a kid. Another of his idols was Buck Williams. "I used to watch Buck play all the time," grins Alaa. "Buck was a god. Now I'm playing with the guy." ▲ Cooper and Alaa tie a horsecollar on an opponent from Phoenix. ▶

Conclusion

Maybe it will be the Portland Trail Blazers and the Chicago Bulls in the NBA Finals in 1992. A lot of Portland fans would be delighted. ▲

It is late July, nearly a month after the Chicago Bulls have laid the Los Angeles Lakers to rest and provided Michael Jordan the opportunity to celebrate his first NBA title. In most NBA cities, after a season that stretches from fall camp in October to the finals in June, fans are taking a break from even thinking NBA basketball.

Not in Portland. A crowd of 21,100 packs outdoor Civic Stadium to watch "Blazer Slam 'N Jam '91." The highlight event is an exhibition game, with proceeds being donated to the offset rehabilitation expenses for Ramon Ramos, a former Trail Blazer who was seriously injured in an automobile accident. There are musical and comedy acts and sky divers and a chance to frolic under the sun on a gorgeous Oregon day. The real reason the masses are paying between $16 and $36 a ticket, though, is that all 12 Blazer players are taking part in the game.

It's a chance for the fans to share one more moment with their heroes. They roar as Terry Porter edges Danny Ainge in the 3-point contest. They form a pathway from the dressing room to the playing court, standing five- and six-deep to get an up-close look at the players as they file by before the game. The fans cheer and shout encouragement and applaud. Some reach out for a touch. Clyde Drexler arrives late with a good excuse—his wife, Gaynell, has delivered their second child two days earlier—and is greeted with a tumultuous roar. This is a party. This is the extension of a love affair like few others in professional sports.

What is it about the Trail Blazers that has so captivated the city of Portland, the state of Oregon and the Pacific Northwest? The Blazers are the state's only professional sports franchise, but there's more to it than that. The region's inhabitants are of a hardy brand, loyal and proud and devoted to supporting their own. They like good entertainment, and for the most part, the Blazers have provided it over the years.

While the Blazers have been the talk of Portland since they won the NBA title in 1977, the unique relationship between the Blazers and their fans has been fueled to an all-time high by the team's recent success. Children, middle-aged men, and grandmothers all have the bug. Lawyers, bankers, grocery-store clerks, longshoremen—the phenomenon known as "Blazermania" runs rampant, and a vaccine has yet to be invented to treat it.

The Blazers accomplished a multitude of things during the past two seasons. They reached the conference finals and made bonafide runs at NBA titles. They established themselves as one of the true powers in the game, a team figuring to be reckoned with in the years to come. They brought national attention to Portland, a city to which such recognition does not come easily.

The future looks good for the Blazers. Owner Paul Allen is willing to spend the money to ensure a strong nucleus of talent. A new arena is in the cards for the 1994-95 season. They'll get their third straight bite at the apple this year. They're in it to win it, and maybe this time, they'll nibble that apple to the core.